HOMILIES FOR FUNERALS

Christ's Death and the Death
of the Christian

HOMILIES FOR FUNERALS

A. M. Roguet, O.P.

Translated by
Jerome J. DuCharme

Franciscan Herald Press • 1434 W. 51st Street • Chicago, Illinois 60609

Homilies for Funerals by A. M. Roguet, O.P. translated by Jerome J. DuCharme from the French, *Homelies pour les defunts*, Editions Salvator, Mulhouse 1975. Copyright © 1981 by Franciscan Herald Press, 1434 West 51st Street, Chicago, Illinois 60609.

Library of Congress Cataloging in Publication Data

Roguet, A. M., 1906–
   Homilies for funerals.

   Translation of: Homélies pour les défunts.
   Includes index.
   1. Funeral sermons. 2. Catholic Church—Sermons.
3. Sermons, English—Translations from French.
4. Sermons, French—Translations into English. I. Title.
BV4275.R6313   252'.1   81-5562
ISBN 0-8199-0786-3   AACR2

Published with Ecclesiastical Approval

MADE IN THE UNITED STATES OF AMERICA

ABBREVIATIONS

Old Testament

Gn	Genesis	Wis	Wisdom
Ex	Exodus	Sir	Sirach
Nm	Numbers	Is	Isaiah
Dt	Deuteronomy	Jer	Jeremiah
Jos	Joshua	Bar	Baruch
1 Sm	1 Samuel	Ez	Ezechiel
2 Sm	2 Samuel	Dn	Daniel
1 Kgs	1 Kings	Am	Amos
2 Kgs	2 Kings	Mi	Micah
Neh	Nehemiah	Hb	Habakkuk
2 Mc	2 Maccabees	Zep	Zephaniah
Ps	Psalms	Zech	Zechariah
Eccl	Ecclesiastes		

New Testament

Mt	Matthew	Col	Colossians
Mk	Mark	1 Thes	1 Thessalonians
Lk	Luke	2 Thes	2 Thessalonians
Jn	John	1 Tm	1 Timothy
Acts	Acts of the	2 Tm	2 Timothy
	Apostles	Ti	Titus
Rom	Romans	Phlm	Philemon
1 Cor	1 Corinthians	Heb	Hebrews
2 Cor	2 Corinthians	1 Jn	1 John
Gal	Galatians	Rv	Revelation
Eph	Ephesians		(Apocalypse)
Phil	Philippians		

CONTENTS

8

INTRODUCTION

Preaching the Mystery of Death

Before the Council

Most textbooks, in chapters devoted to Bossuet, state that death was a popular topic for preaching. The modern preacher or pastor would attest that things have changed, at least in recent years. Funeral sermons are an extinct species. Today, would anyone in his right mind want to repeat those grand celebrations that went on and on, for several weeks, after a funeral?

Not many years ago, preaching on death played a prominent role in parish missions or in "retreat exercises" that reviewed the "eternal verities." In theological treatises, the chapter on the "last things" dealt with death, even though death for the Christian is an intermediate and provisional "end," thus *not* one of the "last things."

How did preachers develop the theme? A nineteenth-century textbook on preaching states it clearly: Arguments from reason, the Bible, Church fathers, etc., firmly establish: 1. All will die; 2. We do not know when death will come.

De la Palice had it all figured out. He disguised the wretched idea content with the draperies of eloquence (the sublime symphony of Henriette of England's funeral oration does no more than orchestrate these two themes) and made practical conclusions, such as: Let us be detached from worldly things; Let us always be prepared to die; and so forth. We can be sure that some Gospel themes were added and, without regard for their true eschatological context, reduced to temporal and individualistic moralism.

At a Centre Pastoral de la Liturgie conference,[1] the conclusion was that the mystery of Christian death is essentially linked with the Easter mystery. Consequently, death can and should be preached during Holy Week, on Easter, Ascension Thursday, the Assumption, and indeed on every Sunday.

13

Although the CPL conclusion can be defended, the recommendation had a major flaw: Preaching death in those circumstances could reach only practicing Catholics; but indifferent or fallen-away Christians, even nonbelievers, come to church for funerals. Isn't that the best opportunity to let them hear the Christian teaching on death?

The latter approach, however, had several problems. It was unacceptable, even for priests who could preach "creative" funeral sermons, to chide unbelieving listeners for their lack of commitment and infringe on their freedom of conscience. Besides, many diocesan regulations advised against the danger of eulogizing parishioners. Then, too, every funeral *had* to be preached, and the funeral Mass had but two readings—and the first (1 Thes 4:13–18) was difficult enough. Much work and imagination were required to vary the theme of funeral homilies that had such a limited scriptural basis.

The Postconciliar Lectionary

Vatican II's Constitution on the Liturgy ruled on just two brief points related to funeral rites.[2] "Funeral rites should express more clearly the paschal character of Christian death." In addition, "the rite for the Burial of Infants is to be revised, and a special Mass for the occasion should be provided." That was not the case when, contrary to the most elemental theology and with no regard for parental grief, custom called for celebration of the votive Mass of the Angels. Most important, the general norms concerning the primacy to be given to God's Word in the liturgical renewal were applied to the funeral liturgy.[3] Thus the English funeral lectionary approved by Rome contained forty-two readings.

The profusion of readings risks putting the priest in an embarrassing position. It rarely happens that a family shows a preference for any text, either spontaneously or in compliance with wishes once expressed by the deceased. To facilitate choice in such an abundant and magnificent repertory, we have provided a section that deals with each pericope at the end of this book: "Useful Notes." We advise which readings could be used for certain congregations and situations, and when such readings should be avoided.

As in my earlier books, *Homilies for the Celebration of Marriage* and *Homilies for the Celebration of Baptism,* I do not use titles from the official lectionary. Instead, I give each pericope a title which, in my opinion, indicates the essential message in the text.

My Commentaries

It is evident that these titles, like "Useful Notes," have a personal and highly subjective value. But how else can I proceed?

Some readers may voice another objection: "Your homilies are generally too long and too complex." In reply, I must say I never intended them to be used "as such"— don't be afraid to adapt and/or develop the homilies. I offer suggestions rather than a text or model. A homily's function is not to comment on every aspect and detail of the scriptural readings. It suffices when the homilist takes a few ideas and expressions from the inspired text, explains them, and applies them to the situation.

Above all, we must seek to interpret the biblical text in the most faithful manner, insofar as that interpretation makes sense in a funeral celebration. But first a word of caution. If we have consulted authorized exegetes on each lectionary text, we should not feel obliged to use all their explanations. The objective task of the biblical scholar differs from the preacher's: the homilist must consider his audience—parents in tears, friends filled with sadness. Little is gained in giving lessons in exegesis, philosophy, or theology. Enlighten the mourners in the faith; give them reasons to hope; invite them to show love toward the deceased by praying as sisters and brothers.

Biblical Doctrine and Catechesis

Homilies for Funerals does not provide a "treatise on the last things"—nor such a treatise transposed in orational style. That would prevent us from accomplishing the primary objective we have set for ourselves: to interpret the biblical text as faithfully as possible.

Because the faith of the Church conforms to scriptural revelation, we can say the Church's current teaching on the last things is not really homogeneous with the Scriptures. The teaching has been "toughened" to some extent, either to meet the needs of elemental catechesis or to eradicate errors that emerged through the centuries.

Take a specific example. You will find nothing on the dogma of purgatory in my commentaries, not even in the reading from 2 Maccabees 7. Although we believe this scriptural passage is the basis for Catholic belief in purgatory, 2 Maccabees 7 does not use the word. Indeed, biblical revelation, in its entirety, does not advocate the static, separate realities which the catechism calls "purgatory," "heaven," and "hell"—not even "particular judgment." The Bible envisions a dynamic order: development of the economy of salvation, which is the plan of God's love toward humanity and its progressive revelation.

I must point out two other important differences between the scriptural and the catechetical or doctrinal presentation of the mystery of death and what lies beyond death. Dogma presents death and "the beyond" as almost independent realities, forming a special division of Christian doctrine. (Besides, the doctrinal viewpoint is primarily individualistic.) But the Scriptures present death as the great enemy of the loving God, who will win in the end. In

16

the New Testament, God's victory over death is realized in Christ, "the firstborn from among the dead." Thus the mystery of Christian death is but one aspect of the paschal mystery, and the theology of the beyond can be renewed only through the renewal of Christology.[4] It should also be noted that the second characteristic of biblical revelation of the beyond is its collective and community aspect.

That does not mean we abandon anything essential in the Catholic belief in the beyond. Take another look at "purgatory." We do not use the word, nor does the Bible. We deal with it as a thing, that is, as an object. But in most of my commentaries I stress that we come together in order to pray for the deceased person, who was, like all of us, a sinner. On several occasions I have even noted the link between the mystery of death and the Eucharist.[5] (Homilists who use my collection for funerals outside of Mass will forgive me for making such a connection and will have to omit those eucharistic considerations.) Whatever the case, the reminder of the efficacy of prayer and the efficacy of the sacrifice of the Mass for the complete solace and liberation of the departed necessarily supposes belief in purgatory.

The Burial of Children

After commenting on the more than fifty-seven biblical pericopes for adult funerals and diverse burial celebrations, I found in the French lectionary nineteen pericopes for the burial of baptized children and a list of thirteen pericopes for unbaptized children.[6] I furnished commentaries for the three pericopes that did not appear in the lectionary for adults. To keep this book within reasonable dimensions, I did not write additional commentaries for the readings common to adults and children; I merely give some brief remarks on homily adaptation for children. These remarks can be found in the second section of "Useful Notes."

17

I think this adaptation is relatively easy by reason of the method I have followed, which is faithful to the Scriptures. Whenever we take an individualistic approach to the mysteries of the beyond, and therefore a somewhat psychological approach, it is difficult to preach on the death of infants. But because death is regarded in the dynamism of the saving plan, which encompasses all humanity, seen as Christ's Body (at least potentially and by vocation), most reflections that I have proposed for adults are also valid for children. They are valid even in the case of unbaptized children. The pessimism which reigned for so long concerning their salvation is less severe today, due to our recognition of God's universal salvific will, Christ's total victory over sin and death, and the Church's sacramental role.[7] Consequently, it is possible to preach for children's funerals, even the unbaptized. No problem exists as long as we show how God's saving plan, in its entirety, confronts the mystery of death.

1. *Le mystère de la mort et sa célébration* (1949 CPL conference) (Paris: Editions du Cerf, 1951). My contribution on the preaching of death is found on pages 349–360. Especially noteworthy is Fr. Congar's explanation of purgatory (pp. 279–336), in particular his last section, on the biblical and patristic sources for the theology of the next world.

2. Constitution on the Sacred Liturgy, nos. 81–82.

3. Ibid., nos. 7, 33, 35, 51, 52.

4. *L'au-delà retrouvé*, Fr. Gustave Martelet's beautiful book (published in 1975 by Desclée [Paris–Tournai]), bears a significant subtitle: "Christology of the Last Things."

5. On this very important and, until recently, much neglected point, see another masterful book by Fr. Martelet, *The Risen Christ and the Eucharistic World* (New York: Seabury, 1976).

6. *Translator's Note:* The English funeral lectionary suggests forty-two readings for adult funerals, thirteen readings for the funerals of baptized children, and three readings for the funerals of unbaptized children. As in the French lectionary for funerals, the English lectionary has some readings common to adults' and children's funerals. Other readings are used exclusively for children. See the Comparison Table (pp. 163–166), which indicates how Fr. Roguet's commentaries can be used with the English lectionary.

7. This is a very brief summary of Dom Edmond Boissard's conclusions in *Réflexions sur le sort des enfants morts sans baptême* (Paris: Editions de la Source, 1974). With convincing accuracy, the first part of the book shows that the "common opinion" which sends unbaptized infants to limbo, is subject to revision, because this "law" cannot be reconciled with any of the following: God's universal salvific will, his love for sinners, the victory of redemptive grace over Satan, and, especially, Christ's universal kingship (p. 71). Inspired by *Lumen Gentium*, I have added to Boissard's list "the Church's sacramental activity" on behalf of the entire human race.

The second part of Boissard's book denies that the magisterium's texts that are usually cited in favor of limbo (pp. 85–123) carry dogmatic weight in the strict sense.

Last of all, it should be noted that Dom Boissard recognizes as theologically important the insertion of a Mass "for the burial of a not yet baptized infant" in the new Roman Missal (p. 131).

HOMILIES:

FIRST READING FROM THE
OLD TESTAMENT

1. Praying for the Dead

(*2 Mc 12:43–46*)

After someone has died or after a funeral, we often hear people say: "It's all over! We'll never see him [or her] again!" We should not be scandalized by such comments. Such words are not necessarily indicators of atheism or materialism. They express what we experience and the great sadness we feel when someone we love—someone who has been a part of our life—is gone. Yes, deep ties are broken. Our everyday life is diminished and mutilated. We experience sadness over our loss, and we are lonely.

Death is indeed a departure and a separation. But it is not a real end or annihilation. We will meet again here on earth, though only in our thoughts. When we die, we leave this world for another world, which is not ours at the present time and to which we have no access as long as we are alive on earth. We cannot even imagine what another world is like.

Christian faith assures us that friends, who are now invisible, are nevertheless alive, that we will join them later, and that even now we can be united with them through prayer. Only our memory keeps us in touch with the past— an earthly past that existed but no longer exists. Prayer, in the mysterious obscurity of faith, helps us attain reality. How so? Because through prayer we reach God, who is not an idea or a memory. God is reality itself, the Great One who exists, the Great One who lives. In God, we rejoin our departed loved ones when we pray to God for them.

Prayer is no dream. It is action—effective and useful action. Prayer allows us not only to recall those we love but to help them and become their benefactors.

About 150 years before Christ, that was the firm belief of a leader of Israel's rebellion against pagan persecutions.

The leader's companions had died in combat. He offered a sacrifice for the full *expiation* of the sins that diminished the glory of God's soldiers.

Today we share that faith. But our faith is stronger and much clearer, since Jesus Christ has come. By his death and resurrection, he guaranteed we will be raised with him. Before dying, he instituted a sacrifice which is far more perfect and efficacious than Old Testament sacrifices. The Mass we offer for those who have left us is that sacrifice.

It is a sacrifice for redemption from sins. It is also a sacrifice of union and communion in the One Loaf, which is the living body of Christ. By the mystery of this bread, we find ourselves gathered together in the obscure certitude of faith as we await and prepare ourselves for our reunion in the light.

2. A Model of Hope

(Jb 14 : 1–3, 10–15)

The Book of Job is a poem about human misery which takes a self-inventory before the impenetrable mystery of God's power. It is also the complaint of a man who has not received the enlightenment and assurances of revelation. But the pagan Job believes in God, his Maker, with absolute certainty.

This perfectly just and charitable man was weighed down with mishaps: the loss of his children, complete ruin, frightful illness. As a believer, Job saw all this coming from God and therefore demanded God's explanation for the injustice.

Obviously, since Job's time our knowledge of God has progressed. First Jews, then Christians, learned from the prophets, and Jesus, that every mishap is not a punishment

God inflicts on us but rather the way God tests us. If we accept our trials, they can purify and enrich us. We know that, and yet when suffering comes into our lives we react "spontaneously," like Job.

Quite naturally, we repeat Job's words: *When a man dies, all vigor leaves him; when man expires, where then is he?* Such questions—yes, even doubts—are very understandable in those who suffer. God himself understands. After all, he allowed the questions and doubts to be in the Bible. Therefore, can't we say it was God who was speaking? He formed our heart, with its weaknesses and aspirations.

But in the depths of his distress, Job did not despair. He says: *All the days of my drudgery I would wait, until my relief should come.* His words sound like those of the De Profundis psalm, which is a psalm of hope: "My soul waits for the Lord more than sentinels wait for the dawn" (Ps 130:6).

Job does not know how his God, whom he believes to be just, *would esteem the work of his hands*—that is, how God would raise up the men and women he has created. Job does not know how that will happen, but in his ignorance he trusts in God and hopes in him.

And we who have heard the Good News of Jesus Christ, will we be less secure in our hope? We know Jesus has died like us and for us, and that we will be raised up like him in order to be with him forever.

The Mass we celebrate is the measure of our hope, because the Mass reunites us, the living, to our dead brothers and sisters in the communion of our Leader's body and blood. Jesus, who was once dead and is now alive, has promised to take us where he is (see Jn 14:3, reading 121).

3. Hope when Hope Is Impossible

(*Jb 19:1, 23–27a*)

When a person suffers deeply and cruelly, when suffering reaches the affections and the body (which are the very reasons for staying alive), it is futile even to try to console with kind words or pious theories. The best we can do is suffer with that person in fraternal silence.

This reminds us of the Book of Job, the ancient writing that continues to be relevant and modern because it is an agonized query into the meaning of life, death, suffering, and misfortune. Job had been taught that a virtuous person is always happy and receives God's reward in this life—but Job, though an upright and just man, was burdened with sadness and humiliations and deprived of all that gave him joy in life. His sermonizing and well-intentioned friends, instead of allowing Job to complain, instead of loving him in silence, heaped advice upon him. They attempted to enlighten Job by repeating arguments that a just God would prefer to have Job acknowledge that his misfortune was chastisement for his sins.

Job turned away from his blundering friends and questioned God with a boldness and familiarity that sometimes seem to scandalize us. But we know that his speech with the All Powerful is an admirable witness of his indestructible faith in God.

Job was a great believer but, like every believer, he believed in obscurity—gropingly—and his distress intensified that obscurity. Still, he believed with all his might. Job hoped in God when hope seemed impossible. Job hoped in the God who afflicted him, in the God whom Job found cruel and unjust.

Nevertheless, Job saw clearly, as in a flash of lightning. Solemnly, he made a stupendous statement: *Oh, would that my words were written down! Would that they . . . were cut in the rock forever!* His words are an act of faith and hope, not founded on reason. Although Job cannot explain their meaning, he has absolute certainty: *I know that my Vindicator lives, and that he will at last stand forth upon the dust.* Unable to know why, Job is certain that this incomprehensible God is alive, that he is the great Living One, who conquers death — that God will have the last word and will, in the end, grant justice to his loyal servant.

This is not just a matter of theory. Job knows that, though he is overcome by evil, he will triumph with God's help: *My own eyes, not another's, shall behold him, and from my flesh I shall see God.*

Quite naturally, we are inclined to see in this last statement an affirmation of the dogma of final resurrection. Job was not ready to admit this, yet he saw (with a faint glimmer) an exception to the ordinary laws of life and death, which he was unable to justify. But for all who suffer, for the afflicted who have a heart-to-heart talk with God, this escape into the future is a powerful encouragement toward lasting hope.

Since the days of Job, believers have made much progress in hope. Ever so gradually, Jews in time of persecution had to acquire faith in personal immortality and resurrection.

Above all, 500 years after the Book of Job, it was necessary for Christ to die and be raised up. He and his apostles have assured us that by baptism we are associated with his death and resurrection. Through the offering of bread and wine, which at Mass become his body and blood, which we receive as nourishment, we carry the seed of resurrection (see Jn 6:54).

Like Job, we can say forcefully (enlightened by graces he could not discern): *My own eyes, not another's shall behold him, and from my flesh I shall see God.* We say this, each one of us, for ourselves and each of our brothers and sisters, and particularly for the person we are burying today, who has gone to be with God, whom Jesus himself said "is not God of the dead but of the living" (Mt 22:32ff.).

4. Does Life Make Sense

(*Wis 2: 1–4a, 22–23, 3: 1–9* [*Long Form*]
Wis 2: 1–4a, 3: 9 [*Short Form*])

In the Book of Wisdom the Bible speaks to unbelievers: *Brief and troublesome is our lifetime; neither is there any remedy for man's dying, nor is anyone known to have come back from the nether world. For haphazard were we born, and hereafter we shall be as though we had not been.*

We must admit that constant and universal experience supports unbelievers. It is quite true that death seems an interruption, a failure, the end of all. And when death takes someone we love, who holds an important place in our everyday life, it helps to be believers, because a disbelieving segment—within each of us—murmurs this temptation: *Haphazard were we born, and hereafter we shall be as though we had not been.*

We have come together to resist that temptation. That's the full meaning of the praying assembly in which we are united at this moment. Common sense, logic, and universal experience, which suggest that life has no meaning, can seem true to a certain extent. But the shortcoming of these arguments becomes apparent if we try to see things from above, by looking, as it were, through God's eyes.

They knew not the hidden counsels of God. Surely you will ask me: "Do you claim to understand God's secrets?" I do not have profound knowledge of them, because I am not God, but I have sufficient understanding through the revelation which the Bible (God's word) and the Church

(God's people) give me. Therefore I can be supported in a faith that makes its journey in obscurity. Without the obscurity, faith is impossible—faith "hopes against hope" (Rom 4:18). The revelation given by God and the Church, the awesome faith I have, lifts a corner of the veil and demonstrates that human life has a meaning which makes it more profound and mysterious.

God formed man to be imperishable. God created men and women, which is another way of saying God has called men and women to be alive. God cannot call the human race to life and to death at the same time. Such a call would be a negation of such life. God, who is Absolute Being, is the great Living One. In other words, God, our Maker, would contradict himself if he were, in his creative action, the Destroyer or the Exterminator. At the same moment, with the same act of his will, God cannot will life and death. When God permits death—tolerates and even blesses death—he does so not to destroy life. On the contrary, death smashes life's limits. Death makes us exchange this earthly life, which is fragile and confining, for an *imperishable* existence.

Someone may object and say that many other beings (animals, for example) have been created by God and have received life from him, and still they disappear in death. The Book of Wisdom provides my response: In creating mankind, *God formed man to be imperishable; the image of his own nature he made him.*

The human race is superior to all other material creatures; nevertheless, men and women are material creatures, and for that reason they must die.[1] The superiority of the human race lies in our unique characteristic of being *formed in the image of God's own nature.* According to the creation narrative (Gn 1:26), that likeness consists primarily in the domination which God's agent, the human race, exercises over every other creature. This implies that men and women have self-awareness, are free in their actions, and are capable of making plans and constructing tools and machines.

But the Book of Wisdom goes further. Created in God's image, man and woman rejoin God in eternity, in the *imperishable* possession of life. Their share in God's eternity is called "immortality." This word is found for the very first time in the Bible in our passage (3:4), some 100 years before the New Testament.

The great mystery that we are God's image cannot be reached only through intellectual reasoning. To *know the hidden counsels of God* and understand his truth, we must place our trust in the Lord, which means we must relate to him as to a father. We must be faithful, rather than allow ourselves to drift away from him by our lack of faith. In short, we must love him, for *the faithful shall abide with him in love*.

For this reason, I repeat, we have recourse to prayer and to the sacrifice of the Mass as a remedy for our heartache and bewildered thoughts, which have been cruelly disturbed by the shock of our loved one's disappearance. Thus we recognize God as the one who grants *grace and mercy*, because he is the everlasting love that gives our life, through death itself, its entire meaning.

5. God Created the Human Race for Immortality

(*Wis 2:23, 3:1–6, 9*)

This passage from the Book of Wisdom begins with faith's categorical affirmation of the real God, our Maker: *God formed man to be imperishable*. That is why in *the image of his own nature God created him*. Our Maker is also our Father. Humanity resembles God as a son and daughter resemble their father. Humanity shares in God's nature and his eternity. Mankind has been created *to be imperishable*.

These great truths, which we believers cling to day by day, may appear to be quite theoretical, quite unreal, when we are faced with the death of someone close to us, because that death seems like a failure or catastrophe. But our sage continues: *The souls of the just are in the hand of God*, which means God's providence takes care of them. This is true of all humankind, especially the just.

No torment shall touch them. The sacred text seems to envision martyrs, or at least those who suffer persecution. But all men and women, though not martyrs in the strict sense, are exposed to torments and trials. Often enough, death comes only after weeks or months of sickness, filled with suffering, humiliations, and distress. But if the trial is accepted, *no torment* shall touch the sick or aged person. On the contrary, the trial produces purification and ennoblement.

The Book of Wisdom invites us to reflect on the mystery of purifying suffering and on the mystery of death, which is passage toward a better life. *They seemed, in the view of the foolish, to be dead*—definitively—but they have only departed. *Their passing away was thought an affliction and their going forth from us, utter destruction. But they are in peace.* This peace is not inert repose, a lessening of life, but an increase in life, a share in God's superabundant life.

Before men, they are punished. That's true: death is a punishment, but not a terrible, hopeless punishment, exacted by an implacable God. Let us be more precise and say death is a penance which puts us to the test, a penance which redeems us and is offered to us by a God of grace and mercy. Most people commit many sins and do hardly any penance for them. But death comes as the supreme penance. Death is the great passover, by which we pass from enslavement and danger to a life transfigured into definitive freedom.

We can also say death is *sacrifical*. God graciously accepts the sacrifice, if tested *as gold in the furnace*, for he recognizes in death the death of his beloved Child, his only

Son. That's why today we offer Christ's sacrifice, the sacrifice of the Mass, so that our friend's death, far from being an annihilation, chastisement, or unending sadness, may be entry into real life in the footsteps of Christ. On the night before he died, Christ said to his Father: "Father, all those you gave me *I would* have in my company" (Jn 17:23, reading 122).

6. "At the Destination in So Short a Time"

(Wis 4:7–15)

We are deeply wounded by a death which seems premature. The Old Testament people, our fathers and mothers in the faith, were even more scandalized by such an event, because they had been told that long life on earth was God's blessing and virtue's reward. Think of the Fourth Commandment in the Decalogue: "Honor your father and your mother, that you may have a long life in the land which the Lord, your God, is giving you" (Ex 20:12; see Gn 25:8, Dt 4:40, Sir 3:6, etc.).

Wisdom, the last book to be written in the Old Testament and therefore the book closest to Jesus, tries to dissipate the "scandal." What, indeed, is "premature death"? Everyone cannot live to be 100 (see Is 65:20). Our hearts are indeed saddened by the departure of such a young man (or woman), with whom we had hoped to live for a good many years. Our hope was that he (or she) would be alive when we die.

But the Book of Wisdom invites us to consider this cruel loss from another perspective. First, let's consider the young person who has left us. Human life is always limited, always broken by death. In this viewpoint, every human life is brief and every death intrusive. Yet it can happen that a very short life has achieved its purpose. Is old age always desirable? Sometimes, it is bitter and sterile. A long life can be empty, but life that *seems* incomplete may have achieved its purpose. Even if it has not produced "important deeds," that does not mean its purpose has not been reached. At the very moment of sudden and unforeseen death, rapid (but invisible) maturation can make one's existence a success in God's eyes: *The age that is honorable comes not with the passing of time, nor can it be measured in terms of years. Rather . . . an unsullied life is the attainment of old age.*

Therefore we must accept God's viewpoint: "The souls of the just are in the hand of God" (Wis 3:1, reading 4). We have to place our trust in his providence, even though our trust is dimmed and saddened. God knows what is good for us. As Jesus tells us: God is a Father, and better than any earthly father, he gives his children what is best for them (see Mt 7:11), even if we do not understand it. By considering how life in this world is often miserable and dangerous, the Book of Wisdom helps us see how a premature death can be, in God's plan, a blessing and the result of his love. *He who pleased God was loved; he who lived among sinners was snatched away.*

Surely, we human beings have a difficult time admitting it: *The people saw and did not understand.* To "understand," we must have faith in God's fatherly goodness: *He who pleased God was loved; he who lived among sinners was snatched away.*

May our shared fraternal prayer—may the sacrifice of the Mass, the great "mystery of faith" which we offer for him who has been taken from our life—obtain for us the grace to believe, despite all appearances, that God is love!

7. God's Victory over Death

(*Is 25:6a, 7–9*)

Unlike us, the people of the Old Testament did not benefit from the Good News announced by Jesus. For hundreds of years, they remained mostly in ignorance concerning what happens to us after death. But in that obscurity (to us this seems almost incredible) they retained a great, invincible hope. God did not make death (Wis 1:13). God is the great Living One (Ps 41/42:3, Is 40:28, etc.). Therefore death, which was introduced into the world by sin (Gn 2:17, 3:19), is God's great enemy. In the end, God will bury death. Our Old Testament forerunners did not know how the victory would occur, but they were absolutely sure of it.

We have the good fortune of having a faith that is more precise and better motivated. But our faith must find its roots in the Old Testament certitudes that are confirmed in the New Testament. St. Paul proclaims God's victory over death (1 Cor 15:54). Some 800 years after Isaiah, the New Testament's last book, the Apocalypse (which means "revelation" of the end time), repeats the very words uttered by the ancient prophet: The Lamb, Jesus Christ, will lead his disciples *to the source of life. The Lord God will wipe away the tears from all faces* (Rv 7:17, reading 68). The New Jerusalem will be "God's dwelling place among men . . . they shall be his people, and he shall be their God who is always with them. *He will wipe away the tears from all faces*; and there shall be no more death or mourning, crying out or pain" (Rv 21:3–4, reading 33).

The life of beatitude in that new world, from which death has been chased, is described by the prophet as an abundant feast which *the Lord God of hosts will provide for all peoples on this mountain.*

Let us not be hasty and dismiss such an image of

heavenly happiness as grossly material. Jesus himself repeated the image several times (Mt 8:11, Lk 13:29, 22:30; see Lk 14:15). In fact, the feast will be a joyous, communal reality. Heaven will be the community of all the blessed. Besides, the feast is prepared by God himself. Jesus announced that he himself will serve us at the feast (Lk 12:37). And because the feast is offered to all, it provides each of us a personal and intimate encounter with God: "Here I stand, knocking at the door," says Jesus. "If anyone hears me calling and opens the door, I will enter his house and have supper with him, and he with me. I will give the victor the right to sit with me on my throne" (Rv 3:20–21).

The Apocalypse speaks in that manner. And the same book contains this exclamation: "Happy are they who have been invited to the wedding feast of the Lamb!" (Rv 19:9). You recognize these words as those used by the priest to invite you to Communion at Mass.

Therefore our Mass is, here and now, the banquet prepared by Christ for his friends. He will begin to dry tears from our eyes by allowing us to share in this rendezvous with God. Here, in the obscurity of faith and the certitude of hope, we are assured we will encounter those who have left us. They have been taken away by death; but in a short time death will be conquered, *on that day*. Then we will be able to say: *Behold our God, to whom we looked to save us! This is the Lord for whom we looked; let us rejoice and be glad that he has saved us!*

8. From Distress to Hope

(Lam 3:17–26)

The Bible brings us God's word. That doesn't mean the Bible is an oracle, dropped from the sky. God's word was written by men who lived, worked, struggled, and suffered, and Lamentations is the work of people who endured the most catastrophic phase of Jerusalem's history. After a year-long siege, the Holy City had been plundered and burned. Its inhabitants starved. Some died and others were deported. The Church gives us the opportunity to hear Lamentations during Holy Week and on an occasion like today, when men and women are deeply afflicted.

Some of us are just about destroyed by this very recent death. Suffering from shock, we tend toward deep depression and pessimism that almost become despair: *My soul is deprived of peace, I have forgotten what happiness is; I tell myself my future is lost, all that I hope for from the Lord.*

Nevertheless, now that we have endured the initial shock, we must resist the temptation to wallow in our *downcast* condition: *The thought of my homeless poverty is wormwood and gall.* Despite our intense sadness, we must be open to hope, and even search for it: *I will call this to mind, as my reason to have hope: The favors of the Lord are not exhausted, his mercies are not spent; they are renewed each morning.* Despite all of life's setbacks and difficulties that create an obstacle to hope, hope can be stirred up and renewed each morning.[2] For the Lord is faithful and *his mercies are not spent.*

Yes, the Lord is faithful. He does not retract his word (see Ps 144/145:13, 1 Cor 1:9, 2 Tm 2:13, etc.). He does not abandon us: *My portion is the Lord, says my soul; therefore will I hope in him.*

We may seem to believe we have nothing to rely on. This is implied in every great loss we suffer. But little by little, in the darkest moments we see a glimmer of hope. Hope grows and turns us toward the Lord as *we wait for him and seek him.* That is the work of prayer: to turn our mourning heart toward the Lord. Just when everything on earth seems to be taken away from us, we turn to him and discover that we are important to him. He will not abandon us, nor will he ever leave us alone.

That is why we gather today with those who suffer great sadness. We can hardly bring consolation to them with our words. Words have a way of irritating rather than calming suffering. Although we are unable to dissipate sadness, as brothers and sisters who are present to each other in prayer and silence we come to this awareness: *It is good to hope in silence for the saving help of the Lord.*

9. Belief in the Resurrection[3]

(*Dn 12: 1b–3*)

The mystery of life after death is one of the most obscure mysteries we face. Therefore it is not surprising that the Old Testament, which for centuries was greatly ignorant of this subject, came to some eventual understanding only after a long, arduous search.[4] Ezekiel's great vision of the dried bones that return to life by the Spirit's power is not yet a revelation of bodily resurrection. It is a parable that prophesied the rescue of the people of Israel.

The Bible's first clear announcement of the resurrection of individuals is in the passage you have just heard, written about 150 years before Jesus Christ. The Jews had been cruelly persecuted by pagan invaders who wanted them to abandon their faith, and many faithful Jews preferred martyrdom rather than deny their faith. We know this from the Books of the Maccabees, the martyrs of Israel. The Jewish resisters died with the certainty that God, for whom they gave their life, would not abandon them in ever lasting death. God would not allow their persecutors to win out in the end. The Jews believed God, their Maker, was powerful enough to raise them from the dead (see esp. 2 Mc 7).

Thus faith in personal resurrection was widespread among fervent believers in the true God. Daniel repeated that opinion and gave it the solemnity and authority of an oracle: *I heard this word of the Lord.*

At that time (that is, at the end of time) *your people shall escape, everyone who is found written in the book.* The *book*, frequently mentioned in later biblical writing, is one of the Bible's images of judgment (see Ex 32:32, Is 34:16, Dn 10:21, Rv 3:5, 20:15). God knows all the actions of men and women. He remembers them and judges each according to his or her deeds (see Rom 2:6–16, 14:12, etc.).

As for those who have died when the Lord comes to judge (see 1 Thes 4:13–17, reading 25), *many of those who sleep in the dust of the earth shall awake. Some* (the faithful) *shall live forever, others* (Israel's persecutors, God's enemies) *shall be an everlasting horror and disgrace.*

Resurrection will not be simply a return to previous life; it will be a glorious transfiguration: *The wise shall shine brightly like the spendor of the firmament.* Jesus will repeat the same image: "Then the saints will shine like the sun in their Father's kingdom" (Mt 13:43).

Jesus' resurrection augments our certitude in universal resurrection. His resurrection confirms and makes more explicit the revelation by Daniel, and sheds light on the agonizing enigma of death.

1. Death, however, is sin's salary (Rom 6:23). But if we abstract from original sin and original justice, men and women were created mortal from the mere fact that they possess a composite and corruptible nature.

2. "My tiny hope sleeps nights in its crib after saying its night prayer. Every morning hope is renewed, gets out of bed, and says its morning prayer with a new outlook."

3. See Gilles Gaide's *Le livre de Daniel* (Paris, 1969), pp. 146–151; P. Grelot's *De la mort à la vie éternelle* (Paris, 1971) ("Lectio Divina," no. 67), pp. 122–124, 181–186; R. Martin-Achard's *De la mort à la résurrection d'après l'A.T.* (Paris–Neuchâtel, 1956), pp. 112–118.

4. The maturation of Old Testament revelation is traced with much expertise and clarity in Sr. Jeanne d'Arc's *J'attends la résurrection* (Paris, 1970), ("Lire la Bible," no. 25).

FIRST READINGS FROM THE NEW TESTAMENT

10. Witnesses of the Resurrection

(Acts 10 : 34–43 [*Long Form*]
Acts 10 : 34–36, 39–43 [*Short Form*])

The encounter with death is always a test for our faith, which risks becoming shaken. But is a comfort to understand how St. Peter presented the Christian faith to a pagan in the early Church. (A pagan, mind you, *not* an unbeliever.) The centurion Cornelius, to whom Peter spoke, was a religious man, sympathetic to Judaism (see Acts 10:2, 22); but Cornelius was a Roman, and Peter wondered whether he could allow this foreigner to belong to Christ's faithful, all of whom were of Jewish origin. And so, with symbolic vision (see Acts 10:9–17, 24–29), God taught Peter that *all* people are called to salvation.

That's why Peter's discourse begins in this manner: *I begin to see how true it is that God shows no partiality. Rather, the man of any nation who fears God and acts uprightly is acceptable to him.* Thus Jesus' Church is open to all, regardless of race, language, social class, or material wealth. *Jesus Christ is Lord of all.*

Peter recalled that everyone in Palestine could see Jesus' public life and miracles, which showed his power and his goodness toward those who suffered. But faith goes far beyond this superficial knowledge of Jesus.

This is the mysterious message that the apostles were commissioned to spread: Christ died on the cross *only to have God raise him up on the third day.* But the risen Jesus was not seen by everyone. God reserved that encounter for *such witnesses as had been chosen beforehand by God*: the apostles, *who ate and drank with him after he rose from the dead.*

Everyone could see the miracles Jesus worked during his earthly life. Only those who believed in him, those who were close to him, witnessed his resurrection and could affirm that he was indeed alive. They were *commissioned to preach to the people and bear witness that he was the one set apart by God* *as judge of the living and the dead,* as we say even today in the Nicean Creed and the Apostles' Creed.

Yes—by his resurrection Jesus has become Master of life and death, *Lord of all,* and consequently the one who judges. We must not let that scare us. Surely we are all sinners, and this makes us fearful of being judged by Jesus, who "alone is holy," as we sing in the "Glory to God." Peter, however, completes his discourse with the reassuring words that echo the message of *all the prophets: Everyone who* *believes in him has forgiveness of sins through has name.*

Thus the first sermon Peter gave to pagans contains the central message of our faith, and can comfort us when we are confronted with death's mystery. *Jesus Christ is Lord of* *all*—the rich and the poor, the wise and the ignorant, the holy and the sinful. He died for our sins and was raised to open for us the gates of true life, life with God.

Jesus is our judge. But first and foremost he is our Savior, which makes him a judge filled with mercy.

The heart of the faith, preached so soon after the birth of the Church, remains faith's essential message for today's Church. We believe that Christ is risen and that by following him, we will enter into real life. It is the duty of a preacher to keep reminding us of Christ, especially when he speaks to people who gather when death occurs.

Such an affirmation may offend those who do not share our faith, but it's true—and the most comforting message we can offer to you today.

11. Christ Has Died for Us

(Rom 5:6b–11)

Though we are certain that every person must die, the death of a person we know and love affects us, wounds us, personally. Death makes us aware that misery and solitude are our lot in life. For our departed brother, as well as for ourselves, death seems to be an interruption, like being torn away. That's what makes death so sad for the person who undergoes it, as well as for those who experience it as witnesses—or, should I say, victims?

In any event, this text from St. Paul should bolster our courage. Yes, St. Paul speaks of death; but in this passage the words "death" and "to die" are applied solely to Christ. Therefore we have a predecessor, guide, and protector on the road that leads to death. But we should note that "death" and "to die" are not used in isolation, in a starkness that makes us afraid. We are reminded that *while we were still sinners, Christ died for us*. Christ died *for us*.

Let us try to understand what "for us" means. Too often we take it to mean "in our place." But if Christ died in the *place* of sinners, in the *place* of men and women, why do people still die, each and every day? Christ's death *for us* means that he died on our *behalf*, for our *advantage*, through love for us.

In other words, Christ gives meaning to our death, which we might otherwise be tempted to consider a torture, an injustice.

First of all, Christ's death *for us* is *proof of God's love for us*. "God so loved the world that he gave his only Son, that whoever believes in him may not die but may have eternal life" (Jn 3:16). And because "God so loved us," Christ died also for God while he was dying for us. And when we die believing in Christ, our death (poor creatures that we are) unites us to God's love, just as Christ's death united him to God's love.

Besides, death enables us to "obtain eternal life." Far from a sign of weakness or an obstacle, death is passage into ever-lasting life, which is God's full, beatific life. Christ's death was followed by his resurrection. Thus we will be *saved by his life*, the life of the risen Christ.

There is yet another word that can bring us comfort, a word repeated three times in this passage: *reconciled*.

We are all sinners, which means we are exposed to *God' wrath*, but God's love is more powerful than his anger. Our faith in Christ and our sorrow for our sins reconcile us with the Father. We would call this into question, if we did not know that God loved us and that he sent his Son among sinful men and women to save them.

Perhaps we wonder whether our dead brothers and sisters did sufficient expiation for all the sins they committed during their lifetimes. But we have good reason to hope that, at the decisive moment, the moment of death's supreme test, our brothers and sisters gave themselves over to God's will in such a manner that they offered their death as a sacrifice capable of achieving *reconciliation*, thanks to *our Lord* Jesus Christ, because he offered himself as a sacrifice for our reconciliation.

12. Through Jesus, the New Adam, We Have Life

(Rom 5:17–21)

Every life ends in death. Our everyday experiences teach us that lesson with constant reminders.

The Bible tells us we have Adam to blame for death. ("Adam" means "man," the one "taken from earth" [*adama*].) Having been taken from earth, every human being must return to earth (see Gn 3:19) as punishment for the sin committed by the first man. This seems unjust to us because we consider each member of our race an autonomous individual, someone who has absolute worth. But, in our "interplanetary age," we are also convinced that we enjoy solidarity with one another in death and in life, in evil and in goodness.

That might make us lose hope. St. Paul, however, wishes to comfort us by reminding us that solidarity in evil and suffering is not the reverse of the other solidarity: solidarity in goodness, life, and happiness. If *through one man's disobedience* (Adam's) *all became sinners, so through one man's obedience* (the New Adam's, Jesus Christ's) *all shall become just*—that is, saints: God's friends.

St. Paul calls him a *man* but does not forget that Christ is God. In other words, if Christ were an ordinary man, he would be no better able than you or I to represent, recapitulate, and contain all humanity. But he couldn't do this if he were not also truly human. If he were not human, he would be infinitely distant from us. He would not share in all of human life's miseries, and particularly in death.

Humanity had a first leader, a first father, who brought us ruin. Now, in Christ, we have a new Leader, a new "First Man," who enriches humanity in an infinite way, and St. Paul wants us to understand that Christ's act of reparation surpasses the destructive action of our first leader.

We are all subject to death, but death is like a narrow door that we must pass through to arrive in the world of light, peace, and happiness. *If death began its reign through one man because of his offense, much more shall those who receive the overflowing grace and gift of justice live and reign through the one man, Jesus Christ.*

We have the right to be saddened by death's victory over one of our brothers, which brings us together today. At the same time, however, we have hope that his death is merely the condition for his invisible life, in virtue of the definitive victory that Jesus Christ has won for all who follow him.

13. Baptized in Christ's Death and Resurrection

(Rom 6:3–9 [Long Form]
Rom 6:3–4, 8–9 [Short Form])

To help us understand the mystery of death, St. Paul brings us back to our baptismal mystery: *We who were baptized into Christ Jesus were baptized into his death.*

To come to an understanding of what seems the end of life, we must recall its beginning. In St. Paul's era, baptism was a bath. People were plunged into water. This bath, this descent into water, associates us with Jesus' death, as in death we descend into misery, suffering, and humilitation. But Jesus "came out of it." He returned in the life and light of his resurrection. He did not begin mortal life all over again; he entered into *a new life*, life with God—a life of endless happiness and fullness of glory.

And so *if we have been united with him through likeness to his death, so shall we be through a like resurrection.*

Therefore the death of a baptized person must not inspire sadness in us, much less despair. Death is a passage, not an end: *If we have died with Christ, we believe that we are also to live with him.*

Let us not give the phrase "we believe" the weak meaning it has in modern language: "we think" or "we suppose." Its true meaning is: "We have the certitude that gives us faith." Christ's death is a passage which results in eternal life, the life of happiness with God, in definitive victory over death.

During their lifetime, most baptized people commit many sins and infidelities that separate them from Jesus. Despite these weaknesses (perhaps even betrayals), every baptized person is rooted in Jesus and associated with Jesus' life forever. St. Paul says in another letter: "If we have died with him we shall also live with him. . . . If we are unfaithful he will still remain faithful, for he cannot deny himself" (2 Tm 2:11, 13).

We have gathered together today to pray for this person who has left us. Baptism is the reason why we can pray with faith, with trust and hope. Years ago, baptism united this child of God with Christ, the Firstborn from among the dead (Col 1:18). He who has died will be united to the risen Christ, the first of all those risen from the dead (1 Cor 15:20, see readings 19 and 20). Christ wishes *all* the baptized to follow him into risen life.

14. We Are God's Children

(Rom 8:14–17)

A member of our believing community has just died, and we are filled with pity and sorrow. We are tempted to quote the poet who said: "The dead, the poor who die, have the greatest suffering."[1] They have suffered a great deal during their life and they have suffered much in dying, and now they seem to be lost, deaf, mute—gone forever.

Christian belief will dissipate this very understandable anguish, over human compassion. Our faith reminds us that baptism gave us *the Spirit of God;* who makes us God's sons and daughters: *Led by the Spirit of God, we have a spirit of adoption through which we cry out, "Abba!" (that is, "Father").* This is how Jesus called upon his Father in his native language (MK 14:36).

"Abba" is a familiar, childlike term which has the warm translation "Daddy," rather than "Father." We can and we should speak to God with such simplicity and tenderness, because *the Spirit himself gives witness with our spirit that we are children of God.*

Faced with death for ourself and for our departed brothers and sisters, we must have the simple, quiet trust that a small child has in his father. That is why the ritual for Christian burial uses the "Our Father" at the wake, at the cemetery, and at the funeral Mass.

When we say "Our Father," we include in the "our" both the living, who say the prayer, and the person for whom the prayer is offered. In the remainder of the prayer, we intend to place in our Father's hands the person he has just called to himself. We ask the Father to allow the deceased to enter into the kingdom which is to come, to give the deceased the bread of the ever-lasting day (in which he will live from now on), and to pardon his sins and deliver him from all evil. Let him enter into God's reign.

St. Paul has just told us: *We are children of God. But if we are children, we are heirs as well.* A father wants his children to possess his wealth, his happiness, and his life; and we are introduced to that inheritance in death. Although the face which death presents on earth is filled with tears and sadness, the face which death presents to God shows much tenderness, the Father's tenderness.

Yes, death is sorrowful. It leads us to *suffer with* Christ *so as to be glorified with him.*

15. There's a New World Coming

(Rom 8: 18–23)

Whenever our life is touched by the death of a parent or friend, we are not only wounded by the loss of that unique person. The whole world seems to be absurd, and life seems to have no meaning. St. Paul concedes that, due to human sin, all *creation* is *subject to futility* and to *slavery*, the inevitable *slavery to corruption.* At the same time, St. Paul turns us away from total pessimism because he describes merely the temporary state of creation.

Universal suffering is *not without hope* (as opposed to dismal, fatalistic resignation), and testifies that we refuse to admit annihilation as our unavoidable destiny. Death's somber door opens into light. What we suffer are the pains of childbirth. *All creation groans and is in agony even until now,* and prepares our adoption as God's sons and daughters and *the redemption of our bodies.*

In the true, Christian perspective, death is not the body's liberation from prison, an escape from matter, which is considered to be evil. Certainly, the body is destroyed through death, but only in a provisional way. The soul, despoiled of its body, possesses another mode of presence to the world and to its sisters and brothers. This manner of being present, which defies our imagination, is only transitory. Slowly but surely, and ever so arduously, through human work, suffering, and love are born the new heavens and the new earth announced by the prophets (Is 65:17, 66:22; in the New Testament, Acts 3:21, 2 Pt 3:13, Rv 21:1–5).

Then indeed we will receive the complete *redemption of our bodies,* their total freedom, because they will be entirely free from the limits and constraints of death and sin. And that will be not only deliverance and happiness for each one of us, the "salvation" that we too often envision as a purely individualistic, even egotistical accomplishment. Simultaneously, that liberation will be our reunion, our reinsertion into that new earth on which we will share in God's reign—that is, in his happiness and life.

Jesus consoled the apostles, who were saddened by his approaching death, by telling them the parable related to the images used by St. Paul: "When a woman is in labor she is sad that her time has come. When she has borne her child, she no longer remembers her pain for joy that a man has been born into the world." Jesus goes on to say: "In the same way, you are sad for a time, but I shall see you again; then your hearts will rejoice with a joy no one can take from you" (Jn 16:21–22).

The apostles will indeed see Jesus, and their hearts will rejoice when he is risen. His resurrection makes Jesus the conqueror of death and sin. Besides, his resurrection inaugurates and guarantees *our* future resurrection and the final restoration of the entire universe, for "in him everything in heaven and on earth was created. . . . All were created through him and for him . . . in him everything continues in being. . . . It pleased God to make absolute fullness reside in him" (Col 1:16–19).

Christian realism, quick to recognize the cruelty of suffering, helps us discover that suffering is a "draft copy" for a renewed universe. Thus St. Paul began his words to us: *I consider the sufferings of the present to be as nothing compared with the glory to be revealed in us.*

We are here, my sisters and brothers, to hear God's word and to nourish our faith. We are here to pray, which means we put our convictions into action by interceding for our departed brother in order to have his deliverance more rapid and more complete. Through that process, we allow sorrow to stimulate and support our hope, because hope must have the last word: "The mystery of Christ in you, your hope of glory" (Col 1:27).

16. "Who Will Be Able to Separate Us from Christ's Love "

(Rom 8:31b–35, 37–39)

What distresses and shakes us in the death of one we have known and loved is not just that he or she has left us and now we are separated during this life. Even more profoundly, every death seems to us to be a failure of love.

St. Paul, on the contrary, proclaims death as a victory of love. What a paradox! How can he have that conviction? He has just told us, but in a somewhat disguised, somewhat mysterious manner.

Let me explain, The basis of Paul's argument is that Jesus' death is the model and prototype of every Christian's death. Jesus is "the firstborn of the dead" (Col 1 : 18, Rv 1 : 5). And that exemplary death of his is a testimony of love toward us, first of all, on the Father's part: *He did not spare his own Son but handed him over for the sake of us all*, because "God so loved the world that he gave his only Son" (Jn 3 : 16).

And Jesus, his Son, died in obedience to his Father (Jn 10 : 18, 14 : 31), through love for his Father (ibid.) and through love for us: "There is no greater love than this: to lay down one's life for one's friends" (Jn 15 : 13), as Jesus himself said. In the words of St. Paul: "The Son of God . . . loved me and gave himself for me" (Gal 2 : 20).

Jesus' death, however, was not a failure or a loss, but a victory: a conquest of life in its fullness, because *Jesus, who died . . . and was raised up . . . is at the right hand of God and intercedes for us.*

That is why nothing *will separate us from the love of Christ. We are more than conquerors because of him who has loved us.* Nothing, *neither death nor life, nor any other creature, will be able to separate us from the love of God that comes to us in Christ Jesus, our Lord.*

Perhaps you will say: "And what about our sins?" True, sin can separate us from God's love. *Only* sin can separate us from God's love. But the Father and Jesus have loved us precisely because we are sinners. "The Son of Man has come to search out and save what was lost" (Lk 19 : 10).

The deceased, in whose memory we gather, was surely a sinner, as we all are. But by baptism he was forever incorporated into Christ. He was able to repent of his sins, and make up for his sins, by a little love which, united to God's love, becomes an infinite love. Finally, he was able to reconcile himself completely with God by accepting, with total confidence, the supreme test of death, the total sacrifice God proposes to us when he calls us to die.

Therefore with trust we commend our brother to *Jesus, who died and was raised up and is at the right hand of God,* where he *intercedes for us.*

17. We Belong to the Lord

(Rom 14:7–9, 10b–12 [Long Form]
Rom 14:7–9 [Short Form][2])

The common practice or attitude is to look at each person's life and death as something strictly personal. With regard to life, this common attitude is "minding one's own business" or "living one's own life." With regard to death, it seems obvious that each of us dies alone, without anyone's being able to turn death aside or accompany the dying person in that great passage.

Christianity sees things differently, as we have just heard St. Paul say: *None of us lives as his own master and none of us dies as his own master. While we live we are responsible to the Lord, and when we die we die as his servants. Both in life and in death we are the Lord's.* And St. Paul gives us the reason: *That is why Christ died and came to life again* through resurrection, *that he might be Lord of both the dead and the living.*

That is a doctrine St. Paul held firmly and often mentioned in his letters. "Christ died for all so that those who live might live no longer for themselves, but for him who for their sakes died and was raised up" (2 Cor 5:15).[3] Paul says of himself: "I died to the Law [of Moses]," which seemed to

Paul, a Jew by birth, the guarantee of salvation, in order "to live for God" (Gal 2:19).

Jesus had already said the same thing about the dead: "God is not the God of the dead but of the living. All are alive for him" (Lk 20:38). Even more radically, St. Paul will say: "Christ will be exalted through me, whether I live or die. For me, 'life' means Christ; hence dying is so much gain" (Phil 1:20–21), because in dying he (and we) will be even more alive with Christ.

In response, you will tell me that this total giving of self to Christ in life and in death, this fusion, this perfect identification, is reserved for the great saints: a St. Paul, a St. Francis of Assisi, a St. Therese of Lisieux.

It is true that we are sinners—mediocre, eaten away by selfishness, distractions, and lost time. Nevertheless, St. Paul's words apply even to us. In fact, St. Paul told us that our belonging to Christ is Christ's initiative, not ours: *Christ died and came to life again, that he might be Lord of both the dead and the living.* It is he who first loved us, who died for us and has become our Firstborn, our Leader, whether we like it or not.

Through baptism, he consecrates us to himself, and this baptismal consecration is not effaced even by our subsequent sins, as St. Paul says: "I have been grasped by Christ Jesus" (Phil 3:12–14). Surely we in turn must try to "grasp" him.

Aside from those who have consecrated their whole lives to God, how many average Christians at certain decisive moments—when getting married, when faced with hardship, when they have given of themselves in service—have truly oriented their lives toward the Lord and not toward their own self-centered satisfaction? But because death is the crown of every life, and gives life its ultimate meaning, how do we know whether a life, which appeared very average, has not been entirely consecrated, at the end, through an acceptance of death that has revealed the profound meaning of a life which had seemed so insignificant?

We are here with confidence to implore Jesus, who is *Lord of both the dead and the living.*

However, St. Paul's text concludes with a reminder of judgment: *We shall all have to appear before the judgment seat of God. . . . Every one of us will have to give an account of himself before God.*

Doesn't that epilogue, death, make death frightening for believers? It does. But we must not forget that Jesus has been constituted "judge of both the living and the dead," because of his death and resurrection, which have made him, we repeat, *Lord of both the dead and the living.* He judges not only "with justice" but also with love and mercy those whom he has come to save (see Acts 10:42–43, 17:31, 1 Thes 1:10).

"God did not send the Son into the world to condemn the world, but that the world might be saved through him. Whoever believes in him avoids condemnation" (Jn 3:17–18).

18. The Good News

(1 Cor 15:1–5, 11)

Whenever we learn of the death of a friend, a contemporary, a relative, it is always sad news, bad news. But today St. Paul reminds us *of the Good News, the gospel, which you have received.* In fact, the word "gospel" means "good news," "glad tidings."

In just a few words, St. Paul expresses the faith he holds. His words are a Christian formula of faith, a kind of catechism answer, the oldest that has come down to us. It dates from A.D. 55, twenty-six years after Christ's death.

Here is the summary of that Good News: *Christ died for our sins in accordance with the Scriptures, and he was buried*, which shows the reality of his death. St. Paul didn't have to prove Christ died. Everyone knew that fact. Being truly human, Christ died. But how does that contain the Good News?

The Good News is that *he was buried, in accordance with the Scriptures*. That means his death was neither an accident nor an everyday event; neither a failure nor a great hope dashed to the ground. His death is a victory over evil because it removes all our sins. The proof is that *he rose on the third day*, again *in accordance with the Scriptures*.

That sentence, which is twice repeated, does not necessarily mean all that had been foretold by the Old Testament prophets and psalms. The meaning is that Jesus Christ's death and resurrection are the completion and realization of God's entire plan, revealed by the Scriptures—namely, to obtain the salvation of all humankind through Jesus Christ's passover.

Paul didn't have to prove that Jesus was truly risen. Paul merely had to recall that Jesus appeared to Peter, then to all the apostles and to the disciples—many of whom were still alive (verse 6). All anyone had to do was question them. They had seen the risen Lord.

For centuries, the Jews had not found the certitude of personal survival beyond death in the Scriptures. Resurrection was even less certain. We see some notion of resurrection in the last books of the Old Testament: Daniel, the Martyrs of Israel or Maccabees, Wisdom. We find in the prophets and psalms a sureness of living forever with God (see Ps 15/16, 22/23, 90/91, etc.), and belief in God's final victory, but Christ's coming and the certitude of his resurrection were needed to dissipate all obscurities. That's the Good News which St. Paul recalls for the Corinthian Christians and for us today, so that we can find comfort.

Therefore the essence of our faith is that Christ, our

Model and Leader, died as we do. But he died *for* us, and his death is the cause of our salvation. He also triumphed over death by being raised from the dead, and his resurrection also concerns us. Christ's resurrection announces that we, like Christ, will be raised in order to be with him. That is our faith. That is our hope. That is the Good News—the Gospel by which *you are being saved*.

19. With Christ We Will be Raised Up

(*1 Cor 15:12, 16–20*)

When someone we love, someone close to us, is taken away by death, we say we have "lost" that person. And we get the despairing impression that the loss is definitive and that death is really an end. Therefore we are quick to say we have suffered "an irreparable loss."

That's true, as far as life in this world goes. But Christian faith assures us the contrary is true, by affirming that the dead will be raised up. We say it in the Creed: "I believe . . . in the resurrection of the body and life everlasting" (Apostles' Creed). "We look for the resurrection of the dead, and the life of the world to come" (Nicean Creed).

St. Paul reminds the Corinthians of this belief because the Greeks thought resurrection of the dead was impossible. When St. Paul had spoken to the Athenians about it, they had ridiculed him and put an end to his discourse with these words: "We must hear you on this topic some other time" (Acts 17:32).

Like the people of Athens, we are quick to admit the soul's immortality, which seems to be a logical consequence of its immateriality. But isn't *bodily* resurrection a miracle? What purpose would it serve? Isn't it essential that only the soul be saved?

St. Paul cannot admit this. He was speaking to Christians, people who believed in Christ, who believed that the Christ who died on Calvary is alive forever (see Acts 25:19). Besides, Christians believe that Jesus is their Leader and that he opened for them the gates of eternal life, which is life with God. Thus there is close solidarity between Christ and Christians. Jesus said it himself: "This is the will of my Father that I should lose nothing of what he has given me; rather that I should raise it up on the last day" (Jn 6:39, reading 115). And on the night before he died, he prayed: "Father, all those you gave me I would have in my company where I am" (Jn 17:24, reading 122).

If we doubt the resurrection of the dead, St. Paul says, it's because we don't really believe in Christ's resurrection, for his resurrection is not an isolated miracle or a reserved privilege. Christ's resurrection is the seed and beginning of the resurrection of all men and women whom Christ encompasses, recapitulates, and leads into his Father's kingdom. Denial of the resurrection of all humankind means the denial of Christ's resurrection, which is the very core and basis of the entire Christian belief. Without resurrection, our faith would be inconsistent and amount to no more than a flighty daydream: *Your faith is worthless. You are still in your sins.*

Christ's resurrection is the sign of his victory over death and sin. Otherwise, *those who have fallen asleep in Christ*—yes, even they—*are the deadest of the dead.*

The risen Jesus is not an impalpable, invisible being or "spirit." He said to his disciples on Easter Sunday: "Look at my hands and my feet; it is really I: Touch me, and see a ghost does not have flesh and bones as I do" (Lk 24:39).

"It is really I!" The body becomes part of the identity and personality of each of us, as was the case with Jesus, God's incarnate Son, who took on our human nature.

Therefore if we are raised in our flesh, we will discover

ourselves completely whole. We will recognize ourselves. We will not be *still in our sins*.

That is why we maintain hope in our affliction. With patience but also with confidence, based on God's Word, "we look for the resurrection of the dead, and the life of the world to come."

20. The Final Victory over Death

(*1 Cor 15*: *19–24a, 25–28* [*Long Form*]
1 Cor 15: *19–23* [*Short Form*])

Although unbelievers reject the revelation and truths taught by Christianity, quite often they acknowledge a definite moral value in Christianity. They see that Christianity provides principles for order and a basis for recognizing the dignity of the human person. That is the opinion we hear in the often quoted words of Montesquieu: "How admirable! The Christian religion, which seems to have as its sole object happiness in the next life, succeeds in making us happy even in this life."[4]

Montesquieu's eulogy is ambiguous, perhaps even ironic, and St. Paul would have wanted no part of it. He implicitly contradicts Montesquieu in the reading you have just heard: *If our hopes in Christ are limited to this life only, we are the most pitiable of men.* If that were the case, death would be a great misfortune for us and a definitive separation. For God himself, human death would be no more than a failure that cannot be corrected.

But as it is, St. Paul claims, *Christ has been raised from the dead, the first fruits of those who have fallen asleep*, in order to lead us into resurrection, *at his coming*. That is exactly what our Creed says: "On the third day he rose again . . . and will come to judge the living and the dead"—that is, all men and women, those who died before his return and those who are still alive on that great day. Our Creed concludes: "We look for the resurrection of the dead, and the life of the world to come," which Christ will inaugurate on his return.

Certainly, because of human nature and as a consequence of sin, all men and women are mortal. We have inherited that from the first man, the head of our race. But when Christ came on earth and became man, he picked up fallen human nature in his hand—if I can use such a description—and delivered humankind from sin and death, which is "the wages of sin" (Rom 6:23). Christ is risen as *the first fruits*, but *then* he will raise up *those who belong to him*, those who became united with him through faith and baptism, *at his coming*. Therefore we understand why the early Christians had a favorite prayer, which we too must repeat with hope in our hearts: "Come, Lord Jesus!" (1 Cor 16:21, Rv 22:20).

The great day of Christ's return will be the day that ends history: *When finally all has been subjected to the Son.* Jesus said while dying on the cross: "Now it is finished" (Jn 19:30, reading 130). Even though everything had been fulfilled in principle, the need remained to fight the battle for salvation of all humankind. That's the same battle we wage here on earth against death and sin, in which we sometimes seem to be defeated. But in an invisible way, Christ battles on our side and will make us victorious. That's one of the meanings of the "Christ the King" title, which we sometimes understand so poorly.

Christ is King of the human race, now in the process of suffering and struggle. But the battle will end with a definitive victory over death and sin. Thus the petition we make in the Our Father will be fulfilled: "Thy kingdom come." The Son's reign as head of humanity will be completed. As man,

Christ will place humanity again in subjection to the Father. As God, equal to the Father, Christ will reign with him.

The last enemy to be destroyed is death, the death that wounds us and tests us today. The victory will be complete and definitive. And thus St. Paul concludes with a magnificent phrase, portentous but simple: *So that God may be all in all.*

We cannot imagine a more beautiful definition of sheer heavenly joy. God, who today seems to us distant, silent, and obscure, will be very near and evident. We will communicate with him without intermediary or eclipse, without fear of being separated from him. He will be our eternal happiness. We will be filled with God. Think of that: the infinite God will not be before us, or even nearby—he will be *in* us and we will be *in him*.

And because he will be *all in all*, we will communicate with each other in him. No longer will there be separation or distance. We will bask in the same happiness. We will be happy, not only because God will be in all of us, but also because we will find that we are happy with each other in a perfect and definitive unity.

21. We Will Be Raised in a Transformed State

(1 Cor 15:51–54, 57)

We have just heard the conclusion of a long development in which St. Paul wished to persuade his Corinthian faithful (we too can heed this ever-living word today) concerning the dogma of the resurrection of the dead, of all the dead, at the end of the world. That will occur when Christ "will come to judge the living and the dead," as we attest in the Apostles' Creed. St. Paul rests his certitude on Christ's resurrection, the center and foundation of all Christian belief.

It is quite certain that St. Paul announces to us a *mystery* that surpasses all we can imagine. He does not tell us—he cannot tell us—how that will come to pass. First of all, Paul is satisfied to affirm that it will be the work of God, who has created everything. God created bodies, plants, the stars in all their beauty and diversity (verses 35–41).

In the same passage, St. Paul warns of two errors that would create in us an entirely false and undesirable notion of our future resurrection.

All of us are to be changed—in an instant,[5] not as the effect of a natural evolution, as happens when a wheat grain, planted in the earth, grows to be a mature wheat stalk, a comparison St. Paul used earlier (verses 37–38). Bodily resurrection will be instantaneous, because it will be the Creator's supernatural work.

We shall be changed; that is, we will not return to our former life. It would not be worth the bother of resurrection if it meant a return to our earthly misery: *This mortal body must be clothed with immortality.*

We will not be raised like the dead people Jesus miraculously raised during his lifetime. Those people ended their earthly life, as everyone does, by dying.

Our body will not be reconstructed but transformed—glorified and divinized.

Nevertheless, we will not become like angels, who are immaterial and unreachable creatures. We will indeed be human. Our body, which designates and identifies us, will be revived. And consequently we will recognize ourselves.

We will not be lost or confused in a vague, general immortality. We will not be lost to a God who has refused to respond to our deep desire to live in him while we remain ourselves, with all our best qualities.

Thus death will be *swallowed up in victory*. God, through Jesus Christ, will accomplish a full and definitive victory over death and sin, which have made our earthly life so precarious, fragile, and wretched.

St. Paul concludes joyously: *Thanks be to God who has given us the victory through our Lord Jesus Christ.* That's what we will be doing in our celebration of Mass. The Mass is not only supplication for the deliverance of the deceased, but also "Eucharist," that is, "thanksgiving" for all God has given us of certitude and hope *through our Lord Jesus Christ.* In fact, at Mass Jesus becomes present in his risen condition. Personally victorious over death, he makes himself our thanksgiving, and by Communion he plants in our body his risen body as the seed of our resurrection (see Jn 6:51, 54, 58).

22. Death and Transfiguration
(*2 Cor 4:14–5:1*)

The message St. Paul just addressed to us is encouraging: *God who raised up the Lord Jesus will raise us up along with Jesus.* And that resurrection will result in the reunion of those whom death has separated. Thanks to the final resurrection, God will provide for us *a dwelling in the heavens* with Jesus.

Paul's outlook on the future should help us get through the present trial, which consists in more than death. Frequently, death is preceded by a long or painful period of weakness and physical deterioration. With the exception of the young, everyone experiences the effects of age and fatigue. St. Paul compares us to a house that gradually deteriorates and falls apart. But he assures us that, at the same time, we are an invisible house that is being constructed?

A better description might be that we are a house being renovated and rejuvenated. From the outside, we see in the suffering person only weakness and the gradual disappearance of his abilities, but such a person can be reborn through his suffering and humiliation, which unite him intimately with our Lord's passion. That's the meaning of the very comforting (though somewhat mystifying) words: *We do not lose heart, because our inner being is renewed each day even though our inner being is being destroyed at the same time. The present burden of our trial is light enough, and earns for us an eternal weight of glory beyond all comparison.*

That's something we must believe in even if we don't see it. Therefore we must not allow ourselves to be weighed down by recalling the sad end of the person we have lost. Faith must help us discover under those desolate appearances the invisible but real growth of a new person, who slowly sheds a rough exterior in order to acquire a beautiful appearance. We can compare the process to a flowering fruit tree, which, although its blossoms die and fall off, prepares shiny and tasty fruit despite the apparent destruction.

Thus death cannot be reduced to merely its external appearances: gradual weakness and destruction. In reality, death is transfiguration. The person we have seen grow old and wither away becomes, in reality, a new person of imperishable youth: *We do not fix our gaze on what is seen but on what is unseen. What is seen is transitory; what is unseen lasts forever.*

What is seen is our body, our *earthly tent.* And if it must be *destroyed* by death, through dying we arrive at another *dwelling provided for us by God, a dwelling in the heavens, not made by hands but to last forever.* This very encouraging truth is repeated in the first and most ancient funeral preface, in which we thank God in song: "Lord, for your faithful people life is changed, not ended. When the body of our earthly dwelling lies in death we gain an everlasting dwelling place in heaven" (Christian Death I).

23. Toward the Eternal Dwelling Place

(2 Cor 5:1, 6–10)

It is a waste of time to compare death with a departure and to call our dead "those who have departed." Correct terminology helps us avoid words that are too disheartening. The expressions of the truths of our Christian faith must also comfort us in the face of death and give some calm to our distress and fear. For indeed we see the departure, but the destination is an unknown region, filled with mystery for the poor human creatures we are.

St. Paul compares our body to a tent, *the earthly tent in which we dwell.*[6] This tent, a temporary dwelling place, must be *destroyed* by death. Nevertheless, death does not make us vagabonds: *We have a dwelling provided for us by God, a dwelling in the heavens, not made by hands.*

What is this dwelling in heaven? It is our body, raised up by virtue of and in resemblance to the risen body of our Leader, Jesus Christ. Bodily resurrection, which will occur at the end of time but which even now is a certainty, will be God's work, not ours, because bodily resurrection will be like a new creation.

From our point of arrival, St. Paul returns to the departure. He is well aware that there will be a "breaking off," which frightens us, and he wishes to comfort us by showing us what will compensate a hundredfold for death's harsh interruption. To make his argument convincing, St. Paul depicts us as being pulled between two domiciles, two fatherlands, and between two exiles, two situations for "displaced persons" who have neither country nor home.

We know that while we are in the body we are away from the Lord. Not that we are far from him; through grace and love we are truly close to him. But here below, *we walk by faith*: faith is both certitude and blind certitude. *We walk not by sight.*

But, St. Paul affirms twice (verses 6 and 8), *we continue to be confident and we would much rather be away from the body and at home with the Lord.* We accept the fact that we are expatriated by death. We are expatriated from our earthly dwelling; we are repatriated in order to be *at home with the Lord.*[7]

St. Paul concludes with a word to us, the survivors. His teachings are so encouraging and serious that we must reflect on them.

Now, in our exile, we must prepare for our repatriation: all *our aim* must be *to please the Lord.*For what will decide our reception by the Lord will be the judgment that will enable us to be *revealed before the tribunal of Christ.*

Surely that is a fearsome outlook. But we can complete the Apostle's words with St. John the Evangelist's description of love: "God did not send the Son into the world to condemn the world, but that the world might be saved through him" (Jn 3:17, reading 113). "Whoever believes in him avoids condemnation . . . whoever acts in truth comes into the light, to make clear that his deeds are done in God" (Jn 3:18, 21).

St. Paul likewise concluded a similar teaching in another of his letters: "Retain what I have said, and console one another with this message" (1 Thes 4:2, 18, reading 25).

24. Our Bodies Are Destined for Glory

(Phil 3:20–4:1)

One of the realities that most saddens us when we think of death is the fragility and misery of the human body. We have seen the body weaken and deteriorate under sickness. And when the body becomes no more than an inert shell, we entrust it to the earth, in which it will be dissolved in the necessary and perpetual cycle of nature's transformation.

Many imagine that the Christian faith considers the body, at best, a simple accessory for human life and, at worse, an unfit burden or obstacle to a full spiritual life. Nothing is further from the truth. Christianity is not a disincarnate spiritualism. On the contrary, it is the religion of incarnation; the religion of God, who became human by taking on a body; the religion of Jesus Christ, a man like ourselves, who suffered all our trials, with the exception of sin (Heb 4:15). Christianity is the religion of the redemption—that is, our total liberation, brought about by Jesus' bodily death and resurrection.

Our body is the instrument of our sanctification. At baptism the body is bathed; at confirmation our forehead receives the laying on of hands and anoiting with oil; through the Eucharist, it is the body that is first nourished by Christ's Body and Blood. Finally, the Church's sacrament of anointing, designed for sick bodies, consecrates them for collaborating in the world's salvation through the body's union with Christ's passion. That bodily anointing is accompanied by prayers to obtain the healing of the body. Our prayers ask that God see that the soul is not weighed down by the sufferings or the collapse of its partner, the body.

Before its burial in the earth, the Church surrounds the body with signs of honor and respect. The Church receives the body one last time in Christian assembly and honors it with holy water, which is a reminder of baptism and a sign of purification. The Church also incenses the body, to remind us of its divine dignity, and entrusts it to the earth in a grave blessed by the Church.

All this is quite in accord with St. Paul's brief encouragement, which we have just heard. The Apostle reminds us that we have *citizenship in heaven* through baptism and grace.

From that comes the confidence by which *we eagerly await the coming of our savior, our Lord Jesus Christ.*

Yes, the *Savior* is also the *Lord*, endowed with the *power to subject everything to himself.* He is not only Savior of souls. He petitions the Father for our salvation by reason of his piety and sufferings. And on the last day he *will give a new form to this lowly body of ours and remake it according to the pattern of his glorified body.*

The Church, which likes to pray in imitation of St. Paul's firm hope, tells God in Eucharist Prayer 3 for funeral Masses: "Remember (N) _____, whom you have called to yourself. Since he (she) has been baptized in the death of your Son, grant him (her) a share in his resurrection on the day when Christ, being risen from the dead, will make our poor bodies like to his glorified body."

After St. Paul gave that hope to his beloved Philippians, to whom he was writing, he concluded: *For these reasons, my brothers and sisters, you whom I so love and long for, you who are my joy and my crown, continue, my dear ones, to stand firm in the Lord.*

Christians have *citizenship in heaven.* But that doesn't mean they cease working and struggling on earth, which is their first fatherland. It is on earth that Christians prepare the Kingdom of Heaven. Their hope for resurrection must not be an excuse to escape into revery or nostalgia. Christian hope must help them and us, my brothers and sisters, to *stand firm in the Lord.*

25. The Heaven We Believe In

(1 Thes 4: 13–14, 17d–18)

For us, death seems like the realm of night. Those who have left us seem as though they have departed for another world. They are separated from us by an impenetrable distance. They appear to be swallowed up, as in a dense fog.

Nothing saddens us more than that apparently invincible ignorance that St. Paul was well aware of as he wrote, just twenty years after Christ's death: *We would have you be clear about those who sleep in death, brothers and sisters; otherwise you might yield to grief, like those who have no hope.* By "those" St. Paul means the pagans, for whom death was the soul's flight out of this world. But what can be the life and happiness of a soul that wanders far from its body in an unknown space?

Today, some who hold the Christian tradition seek to be consoled by imaging a sort of geography of the invisible. They represent the kingdom of the dead in this manner in order to communicate with their departed loved ones. But they wish to know too much and seek to overcome the inevitable obscurities that surround all of us who live on earth, in the shadow of faith.

In our materialistic day and age, the majority of people, who admit to only what they touch, will have to be resigned to ignorance. They will indeed *yield to grief*, burdened by the loss of their loved ones, because they *have no hope*. What they say even seems to make sense, because experience supports them: "How can we know what happens after death? No one has ever come back to tell us about it!"

That's precisely what St. Paul refuses to admit! One man, and only One, has come back from the dead to enlighten our belief and support our hope. That man is *Jesus*, who *we believe died and rose*.

Before dying, Jesus said: "I am indeed going to prepare a place for you, and then I shall come back to take you with me, that where I am you also may be" (Jn 14:3, reading 121). And in his most intense prayer, just hours before his death, Jesus said: "Father, all those you gave me I would have in my company" (Jn 17:24, reading 122).

St. Paul relies on the certitude he has from Jesus' words as he concludes: *If we believe that Jesus died and rose, God will bring forth with him from the dead those also who have fallen asleep believing in him. . . . Thenceforth we shall be with the Lord unceasingly.*

Let us examine how sober our Christian belief is. It is not lost in fantastic flights of imagination, which are therefore childish and deceiving. Our faith is a mature faith that tells us what is essential: *We shall be with the Lord unceasingly.* We shall be in heaven—not among pink and blue clouds, nor in a concert of angels strumming harps. On the contrary, heaven contains all our future happiness: *We shall be with the Lord unceasingly.*

Jesus used the same expression to make a promise to a great criminal, who came to regret his faults and to trust in Jesus: "I assure you: this day you will be with me in paradise" (Lk 23:43, reading 111).

That is our Christian belief as we face the mystery of death. I can conclude in no better way than in the words of St. Paul: Retain what I have said, *and console one another with this message.*

26. The Death of the Apostle Paul

(2 Tm 2: 8–13)

We are accustomed to hearing fragments from St. Paul read at Mass, but we don't always listen very well. The text we have just heard deserves our undivided attention, because it is deeply moving. St. Paul gives neither a homily on death nor a funeral sermon. We have just heard the Apostle's last words to his favorite disciple, which St. Paul dictated only a short time before his death, which he foresaw and announced (see 2 Tm 4:6–8).

Not only was the aged Paul alone, which is a source of

sadness for old people, he had been abandoned and betrayed by several disciples (undoubtedly after his trial). Paul's captivity was so strict that a friend who came to comfort him had difficulty finding him (see 2 Tm 1:15–17, 4:9–11, 14–16).

Despite such distress, Paul kept the faith and was supported by this conviction: *Jesus Christ, a descendant of David, was raised from the dead. This is the gospel I preach* — that is, the essential point of my preaching. *In preaching it I suffer as a criminal, even to the point of being thrown into chains.*

Jesus too had been arrested and executed as a wrongdoer. Paul suffered like Jesus and *with Jesus*. As Paul said earlier: "In my own flesh I fill up what is lacking in the sufferings of Christ for the sake of his body, the church" (Col 1:25).

Even at this moment, Paul was convinced his suffering profited the entire Church: *I bear with all of this for the sake of those whom God has chosen, in order that they may obtain the salvation to be found in Christ Jesus and with it eternal glory.* Therefore the suffering Christian becomes one with Jesus Christ and obtains *salvation and with it eternal glory.* The same Christian obtains salvation for his sisters and brothers in virtue of the communion of saints.

Paul is in chains, *but there is no chaining the word of God!* The word will continue to spread, through the mission of Paul's followers, such as Luke and Timothy, and through Paul's sufferings and death, united to Christ's sufferings and death.

Far from being a loss, the death that saddens us today may have a productivity and radiance that go far beyond our expectations.

St. Paul was strengthened by something he could *depend on*, something worthy of trust, which also pertains to apostolic preaching: *If we have died with him*—our baptism has truly enabled us to die with him — *we shall also live with him*; we shall be associated with his resurrection (see Rom 6:3–5). *If we hold out to the end, we shall also reign with him.*

Jesus had promised his disciples: "Whoever acknowledges me before men I will acknowledge before my Father in heaven. Whoever disowns me before men I will disown before my Father in heaven" (Mt 10:32–33). Paul echoes the same threat: *If we deny him he will deny us.*

But Paul is quite certain that he has not denied his Master: "I have fought the good fight, I have finished the race, I have kept the faith" (2 Tm 4:7). Is that pride? No. Paul also knows he is a sinner, like the rest of us, like the person we are praying for.

But having faults, even grave faults, is one thing. To *deny* Jesus is an entirely different matter. Paul also concludes: *If we are unfaithful* . . . The parallelism in the passage might make us think of the previous statements: "the Lord will be unfaithful to us." But no! Such logic is overturned by the love of God, who cannot be defeated by our weaknesses.

Paul concludes with a triumphant affirmation that must remain our strength in our mourning: *If we are unfaithful he will still remain faithful; for he cannot deny himself.*

27. Joy in Time of Trial

(1 Pt 1:3–8)

We have come together to share our grief and sorrow. And lo and behold, we hear a page from St. Peter, a page that shimmers with joy. Isn't that surprising, perhaps shocking? It is *not*, because St. Peter is addressing Christians, who are tested by persecution but find their strength in the assurances their Christian faith gives them.

I hope that you share the faith and the comfort it brings.

For those of you who may not believe this, I respect your position. Nevertheless, I ask everyone to consider how our faith answers the questions asked of us by the human condition.

St. Peter begins with a benediction, as we find in most Jewish prayers: *Praised be the God and Father of our Lord Jesus Christ.* Peter immediately indicates the motive for this rejoicing: *in his great mercy*—his paternal tenderness for our misery—*he gave us a birth unto hope which draws its life from the resurrection of Jesus Christ from the dead. He gave us a new birth.*

That expression, which has a very precise meaning, deals with baptism, which is correctly called the sacrament of new birth (see Jn 3:3, 5, Ti 3:5–7). Baptism has incorporated us into Jesus' death. Thus for a baptized Christian the earthly death that we mourn today consists in dying with Jesus Christ. But baptism also implies (see Rom 6:3–11) that the Christian can say with St. Paul: "I wish to know Christ and the power flowing from his resurrection; likewise to know how to share in his sufferings by being formed into the pattern of his death. Thus do I hope that I may arrive at resurrection from the dead" (Phil 3:10–11).

Resurrection is not a resumption of mortal life, a simple rebeginning (which would be extremely sad, because it would condemn us to grow old and die once more). It is being raised *unto hope, a birth to an imperishable inheritance, incapable of fading or defilement*, because the Christian will share in God's eternity, God's eternal youth.

That *hope* is Christ himself, who is "in us, our hope of glory" (Col 1:27).

The *inheritance* is God our Father's kingdom, "prepared for us from the creation of the world" (Mt 25:34). The inheritance *is kept in heaven for you*, like a treasure which no external accident can make us lose (see Lk 12:33).

From this perspective, we understand why St. Peter is so enthusiastic, as he tells us: *There is cause for rejoicing here. You may for a time have to suffer the distress of many trials*—especially the death of those we love. But these trials will test our faith, for it is easy to keep the faith in times of peace and good fortune! In this day and age in which we find ourselves, we must discover how precious is our faith and how it needs to be purified and fortified.

Right now we journey in night. Our faith is but a tiny light, sufficient merely to guide us one step at a time. This faith will be a full light, with no shadow, *when Jesus Christ appears.* At the moment, Jesus Christ is truly invisible, and though we do not see him, we touch him with faith and love. *Although we have never seen him, we love him, and without seeing we now believe in him.*

In conclusion, St. Peter returns to joy. He does not exhort us to joy; he is convinced that the hope he has recalled for us even now makes us *rejoice with inexpressible joy. Inexpressible* because it is hidden beneath our tears.

This secret and mysterious joy transforms us *with glory.* In other words, joy breaks through the veil of sadness and mourning to express the certainty of glory and happiness, the fruits of our baptism.

28. We Are God's Children

(1 Jn 3: 1–2)

If we look at death from a "natural" point of view, we are tempted to criticize God for taking away those we love. We forget that, for all humanity, death is "the wages of sin," as St. Paul says (Rom 6:23). God had willed that we live on intimate terms with him, but human disobedience opposed and distorted that loving plan (see Gn 2:17, 3:19, 22).

We no longer live under that curse. Christians know that God permitted his Son to save us from sin and death. That is why Jesus willed to die. And he gave us immortality by the sacrament that associates us in his death and resurrection: baptism, which makes us God's children by suppressing the original curse.

This is not just a convenient and imaginative manner of speaking. God really shares his divine life with us, just as a father transmits his life and likeness to his children. That's what we have just heard from St. John, the evangelist of God's life and love: *See what love the Father has bestowed on us in letting us be called children of God! Yet that in fact is what we are.*

Obviously, such a truth, such an extraordinary miracle, is accessible only in faith. *We are God's children now; what we shall later be has not yet come to light.*

We must believe in God in order to make that admission, but it is not enough to admit the existence of an Infinite Being, who is our Maker. We must also trust in God's Word and believe that he is a living Person, who loves us in a fatherly way and wishes to give us happiness by sharing his intimate life with us. That is why, St. John explains, *the world*—that is, people distant from God—*does not recognize us.* The world cannot identify us as God's children because *the world has never recognized the Son.*

Unfortunately, we hardly seem to be God's children. We are so mediocre, so selfish, so inhospitable that we convey a meager notion of our Father to people who do not know him and who must discover his resemblance in us. But we have an excuse: We walk in the obscurity of faith. We see God only in a vague way: "Now we see indistinctly, as in a mirror." Only when we die will we see God "face to face." Then, St. Paul says, "I shall know God even as I am known" (1 Cor 13:12). You have surely noticed how similar these words are to what St. John told us: *We know that when it comes to light we shall be like him, for we shall see him as he is.*

For us, death seems like a deep hole, something lost in night. But in reality—we *know* in faith—death is the entrance to a passageway, like a somber tunnel that leads to daylight. If we know how to guard our glimmer of faith, it becomes a great light, a beatifying light in which we will find life and glory. In the end, that light will help us see God directly.

That light will burn away all our imperfections. We will be purified, and able to say with the psalm: "In your light we see light" (Ps 35/36:10). That is why we sing, in the first funeral preface, "The sadness of death gives way to the bright promise of immortality."

29. Love Enables Us to Pass from Death to Life

(1 Jn 3:14, 16–20)

We have just heard a message from St. John, "the disciple Jesus loved" (Jn 19:26, reading 130; Jn 20:2, 21:7). John was next to Jesus at the Last Supper (Jn 13:34, 15:12), when Jesus revealed that he wished to give his "new commandment: Love another. Such as my love has been for you, so must your love be for each other" (Jn 13:34).

John understood that Jesus would give his life for love of us in the sacrament of bread and wine, his Body and Blood, which we are about to celebrate. Finally, John was at the foot of the cross, with Mary, and witnessed Jesus' death, which climaxed with the opening of his heart, from which flowed water and blood, symbols of life and love (Jn 19:25–26, 31–35).

In the text that was read to us today, St. John draws conclusions from the example and precept Christ gave us in his most intense "hour": *We have passed from death to life we know because we love the brothers.* For us, death is nothing more than a "passage." *The man who does not love is among the living dead.* For that person, death is a trap and a dead end. But *the way we came to understand love was that Jesus laid down his life for us. Consequently, we too must lay down our lives for our brothers.*

St. John then calls to mind a person who sees the misery of his brother or sister: *How can God's love survive in a man who closes his heart to his brother?* Impossible! For genuine love is not satisfied with beautiful words. It must be proved *in deed and in truth. . . . This is our way of knowing we are committed to the truth and are at peace with him.*

Those of you who were good friends of the man whose death we "celebrate" today know he was a generous and devoted servant of his sisters and brothers. But surely, like all of us, our friend was a sinner. As St. John said in the beginning of his letter: "If we say, 'We are free of the guilt of sin,' we deceive ourselves; the truth is not to be found in us" (1 Jn 1:8).

We are all well aware of our sins. We readily admit them. But today St. John has uttered that wonderful measage which must rescue us from all fear: *No matter what our consciences may charge us with, God is greater than our hearts and all is known to him.*

Indeed! God knows us in the very depths of our being, even better than we know ourselves. He created us, "He knows how we are formed; he remembers that we are dust" (Ps 102/103:14). God also knows that a multitude of faults cannot prevent anyone from undertaking a deep reorientation of life, sealed by the ultimate gift of death as our expression of love for God and for our sisters and brothers.

As for us, the survivors, we exercise our fraternal love by knocking prayerfully at the heart of the God who *is greater than our hearts.* We pray for this person, who, we believe, is fully *committed to the truth* at this very moment.

30. God Is Love

(1 Jn 4:7–10)

You have heard St. John, the Beloved Disciple, the evangelist of charity, say this extraordinary phrase, unique in all of Sacred Scripture. There is no equivalent in any other religion or philosophy: *God is love!*

But we must admit that the phrase, "God is love," is shocking and paradoxical, and at times seems ridiculous and cruel. It seems to contradict all we see. We see the world God created, the world God declared to be good, filled with battles, destructive forces, and calamities of every kind. And when we are directly touched by death, which may be preceded by much suffering, and which causes so much confusion, emptiness, and uncertainty about the future, especially in the immediate family, we are tempted to think that if God is love, as St. John says, we cannot find enough evidence to support that claim.

That very excusable reaction would have some justification, if St. John and Sacred Scripture referred to God as a "perfect being," infinitely distant and isolated for all eternity in selfish and undisturbed beatitude.

But the God whom Christianity reveals is quite different. He is a living God. Beginning with the Old Testament, we see a God who loves people and wishes to be loved by people, who comes to their rescue and guides and protects them. Later, the Gospel goes much further, to show us that the perfectly holy and perfectly happy God has found a way to suffer in the person of his Son, who is one with God.

That's what St. John has just told us: *Love . . . consists in this: not that we have loved God but that he has loved us and has sent his Son as an offering for our sins.*

We are fragile and limited creatures, whom God could not prevent from suffering. Suffering is both a necessity of our created nature and a consequence of the sin that has stripped us of all the protection God wished to bestow on us in the beginning, when he admitted us into his intimacy. God did not want to suppress suffering. But did he wish to make suffering a good in itself or to give suffering a high value, as some people claim?

In God's viewpoint and in ours, suffering remains an evil. But God's masterpiece, his wonderful invention, has made suffering and death itself an occasion—or, better still, an instrument and language of love and life. *God sent his only Son to the world that we might have life through him.*

No reasoning or argumentation can ever resolve the problem (or "scandal") of evil, suffering, and death. But we can enter into this mystery. We can assimilate the mystery and find meaning in our life if we gaze on the crucified Jesus and offer our own suffering and death, united with his death, in the sacrifice of the Mass.

At Mass, the bread and wine become Christ's Body and Blood. We believe that. We should also believe that, in the existence of a Christian, suffering and death are transformed into love and life.

31. "Their Actions Follow Them"
(*Rv 14 : 13*)

Happy now are the dead who die in the Lord![8] Their death, which may have been preceded by great suffering, is "perfect sleep," provided they have fallen asleep *in the Lord*— provided they died believing in Christ, with childlike trust in their heavenly Father.

"Falling asleep" indicates they will wake up at the last resurrection, but it does not mean they sleep in oblivion and unconsciousness; otherwise we would not call them *happy*.

The Beatitudes, mentioned here and in the Gospel, describe a fullness of life and happiness. Falling asleep *in the Lord* does not mean we give ourselves "into his hands," as Jesus said on the cross (Lk 23:46). "Falling asleep in the Lord" means to join him, to be alive with his life, which is an intense life, not a semi-conscious, diminished life.

In the same manner, *the Spirit added*, "*They shall find rest from their labors.*" In the funeral liturgy we ask that they be given "eternal rest." But that rest is not inertia or passivity. *They shall find rest from their labors*—that is, from all labors, worries, and deceptions that inevitably accompany our earthly existence, because, as Job questioned, "is not man's life on earth a drudgery?" (Jb 7:1). The *rest* described in our reading is activity, because we want not only "eternal rest" for our dead; we also petition: "Let eternal light shine upon them" (see Jn 1:14).

Their life continues, because *their good works accompany them.* Perhaps we might say: "Aren't there a lot of sins among their actions?" Certainly. But sins are only wanderings and deficiencies. Whenever a person dies in the Lord—that is, in faith and charity—the actions which follow that person are surely in accord with his or her fundamental orientation toward the Lord.

We too have an obligation to make sure the *good works* of our dead *accompany them.* We do this when we live up to the same ideal and the same faith, and when we follow them in their dedication and service. We thereby render our dead far more beautiful homage than our "last respects" and our funeral wreaths.

Pascal learned from one of his directors that "one of the most useful and solid acts of charity toward the dead is to do what they would have ordered us to do if they were still in this world."[9] When we pray for our dead and follow their

good example, it is granted that *their good acts accompany them*,
now that they have entered into repose.

32. A New Heaven and A New Earth

(Rv 20:11–21:1)

You have just heard a passage from the Apocalypse or
Revelation, the book Christians generally regard with some
disdain. It has the reputation of being obscure, far fetched,
and terrifying: filled with devastating calamities and catastrophies. In reality, the Apocalypse is a book of hope,
written at a time when Christians were exposed to the worst
persecutions by Roman emperors, beginning with Nero.
Christians were in danger of being discouraged: Hadn't they
been promised happiness when they became Christians?

Even if we do not face the immediate threat of persecution, we can ask the Church, and even God, a similar question. Our human condition is miserable, fragile, exposed to
all sorts of dangers, deceptions, and disappointments. We
sense this in a particularly acute way when death strikes
someone close to us. We are quick to question: "Where is
this Christ I counted on to bless and protect me? Where is
this God in whom I placed all my trust, whom people taught
me to love as a Father?"

The Book of Revelation answers this kind of questioning.
No attempt is made to conceal the agonies, dangers, and
threats of death that assail Christians. But at the same time,
the book reveals ("apocalypse" means "revelation") the
hidden meaning of the combat. Behind the warfare unfolds
immense, invisible war between Christ and his enemies, who
are Satan, sin, and death.

But Christ's final victory over all his enemies—over all
our enemies—is assured, and that must give us encouragement to sustain the sometimes difficult battle waged against
us.

The last chapters of Revelation describe the final triumph, and the passage just read to us belongs to that comforting epilogue.

First of all, there is the Last Judgment. *I saw the dead, the great and the lowly, standing before the throne*, where God will judge them. They are "risen" because we are told they are *standing*. All are raised up: *the great and the lowly*, which is a way of saying "all without exception."

Then *the dead will be judged according to their conduct*. The Apocalypse insists on it: *Each person was judged according to his conduct*. Their actions, inscribed *on the scrolls*, signify God's perfect knowledge of all our actions, even the most hidden. Therefore the so-called general or universal judgment is not a sketchy judgment but a personalized process.

Human justice is at times cruel and lacking in nuance, because its function is to defend society, but God's justice is mixed with his mercy and seeks, above all, to save each person. Didn't Jesus say he came "to seek out and save what was lost?" (Lk 19:10). Therefore those who have heard his word and followed him are inscribed in another book, *the book of the living*, despite the fact that they may have committed errors and serious sins throughout their life.

For the Book of Revelation, only those *whose name was not found inscribed in the book of the living* — that is, those who have fought against Christ and his Gospel of fraternal charity — are excluded from life.

In fact, God manifests his victory over *death* when judgment is rendered. *Death and the nether world gave up their dead*. The human race's slavery to death, which causes so much suffering for us today, is broken once and for all, because *death and the nether world were hurled into the pool of fire*, symbol of *the second death*, from which there is no escape.

Then God himself is freed of death, if I can use the expression. God is freed of the death he didn't create (see Wis

1:13). He is free to bring about a new creation, which nothing will threaten now that death, "the last enemy," is destroyed (1 Cor 15:26, see reading 20).

The author of Revelation goes on to say: *Then I saw new heavens and a new earth.* What we incorrectly call "the end of the world" is in reality the disappearance of a used, worn world, transformed into a new, blissful world that lasts forever: *the new heavens and the new earth,* which were first promised in the Old Testament (Is 65:17, see Is 43:19, 2 Pt 3:13).

That's why the Apocalypse does not intend to scare or attack us. It takes into account the trials that Christians on earth have to endure, but the Apocalypse also gives certainty of consolation, even certainty of final joy.

We may react by saying: "All that is a long way off; we'll have to wait too long for that to happen." In reply, it must be stated that it is already a comfort to know the meaning of these sufferings. It is a comfort, right now, to have our hearts enlightened and strengthened by hope.

But even more should be said. That new and harmonious world, which we wait to see revealed only in the last days, exists today. It is being built. It is growing. We do not see it, but through all our sorrows and trials on earth we share in its construction and growth, because we are related to Jesus Christ.

33. God Himself Will Be With Them

(Rv 21:1–5a, 6b–7)

We have heard a section of the final vision of the author of the Apocalypse. After reminding us of the furious combat that frees the world for God, the author reveals the splendors and bliss that Christians will enjoy in heaven.[10]

Heaven! We seldom hear anyone speak about heaven today. Even its mention provokes a smile. This is surely due to the naive and indiscreet way heaven is discussed, as if someone has gone there and returned with very precise descriptions to inspire a little confidence. Nevertheless, we must speak of heaven, especially when death becomes present. When death touches us in such a deep manner, we must reflect on the afterlife.

We can speak about death with the help of the Apocalypse, a word that means "revelation." Yes, the book uses images, because as incarnate spirits we understand no other language. But we will see that these images are not infantile. Rather than mask and make a caricature of the reality of the mystery of heaven, the apocalyptic images help us explore more deeply all images that are too material in nature.

Our passage begins by suggesting that we are dealing with realities that cannot be expressed and must be entirely imagined. *I saw* (in a supernatural revelation about the final events) *new heavens and a new earth. The former heavens and the former earth had passed away, and the sea was no longer.*

Throughout the Bible, the sea is a frightful element, filled with monsters and dangers that belong to the sinful world, which is in continual revolt against God. Therefore God makes the sea disappear. The same thing happens to *the former heavens and the former earth,* both of which are familiar to us. They are replaced by *new heavens and a new earth*—that is, realities which are unknown to us and which we cannot foresee.

I also saw a new Jerusalem, the holy city, coming down out of heaven from God. It *comes down out of heaven from God,* which means it is God's pure creation. Heaven comes on earth like a *holy city,* which can be compared to *Jerusalem.* In fact, mysterious as it is, heaven is a city, a kingdom, as Jesus often said. This means that we will be reassembled there in perfect peace.

This heavenly image corrects our prevailing notion of heaven as too ethereal, too immaterial, which risks making heaven unreal. Revelation's imagery also corrects our excessively individualistic idea of heaven.

The city's beauty will closely resemble the beauty of the earthly Jerusalem, which inspired great enthusiasm in religious Jews (see Ps 47/48:2, 13; 83/84; 121/122; 131/132: 13–18; 147; and esp. Tob 13:7ff.). Revelation abandons the city image and compares the beauty of the "city of our God" with the beauty of *a bride prepared to meet her husband.* This image reminds us of the freshness and hope of a perfect marriage.

Indeed, heaven will be shown to us as a place where we are with God, and God with us. Therefore heaven is much less a place or location, in a spatial sense, and more a living, personal relationship with God, just as a bride is with her husband, just as two friends are together. "Being with"— that very simple description which frequently recurs in the Bible—has a thousand nuances: *This is God's dwelling among men. He shall be with them and they shall be his people, and he shall be their God who is always with them.*

How else can we think of the God who became man and merited "the name of Emmanuel, which means God-is-with-us" (Mt 1:23)?

This dwelling place with God can produce only joy, and can erase all sadness, as was announced by the prophets of old (Is 27:8, see reading 7). *God shall wipe every tear from their eyes, and there shall be no more death or mourning, crying or pain, for the former world has passed away.*

Up to this point in the passage, an angel has been speaking. Now God himself speaks. He confirms the angel's words as he says: *I am the Alpha and the Omega, the Beginning and the End.*

Everything comes from God: he is the Maker. Everything goes toward him: he is the End. He renews the world and establishes it in its definitive state.

To describe how this state will give a share of divine life, God adds: *To anyone who thirsts I will give to drink without cost from the spring of life-giving water. He who wins the victory shall inherit these gifts; I will be his God and he shall be my son.*

Here on earth, we address God with the words "Our Father, who art in heaven." In heaven we will enjoy the loving intimacy of our Father.

Let us pray to our Father for our departed brother, who is God's child by baptism. May he taste the joy of being intimately *with* his Father, whom he will see face to face.

---

1. Baudelaire, *Les fleurs du mal*: "The generous servant of whom you were jealous. . . . "

2. The selection of verses in this pericope expands St. Paul's thought. He had no intention to present a general explanation of the Christian's life and death, which end in one's appearance before God's judgment seat.

The complete passage (14:1–15:6) concerns a particular case: the relationship between the "strong" and the "weak." The two groups were intermingled in the early communities. The "weak" still see the need to cling to the Law's observance, especially in the matter of eating the meat of sacrificed animals. The "strong" rightfully consider themselves exempt from the Law. "Weak" people must not "judge" the "strong" as being laxists; the "strong" must not "despise" the "weak" as being timorous and scrupulous (see 1 Cor 8:7–13). Let each person live for God, according to his or her convictions, without being preoccupied about others, for "none of us lives as his own master" (vv. 7–9).

Then comes verse 10a (omitted by the lectionary): "But you, how can you sit in judgment on your brother? Or you, how can you look down on your brother? We shall all have to appear before the judgment seat of God." We see that Paul's aim is exhortation: Be indulgent and charitable toward one another. His words on life, death, and judgment (very beautiful and deep) have merely additional, explanatory value.

"We shall all have to appear before the judgment seat of God. . . . Every one of us will have to give an account of himself before God." In this context, Paul invites each person to weigh his own responsibility,

without being preoccupied about others—a frequent theme in the Bible
(Jer 17:10, Ez 18, Ps 61/62:13, Prov 24:12, Mt 16:27, Rom 2:6, 1 Pt
1:17, Rv 2:23). In our commentary, we show this doctrine in its most
general meaning, easily adapted to people who hear such an isolated
pericope.

3. This text is cited in Eucharistic Prayer IV: "In fulfillment of your
will he gave himself up to death; but by rising from the dead, he destroyed
death and restored life. *And that we might live no longer for ourselves but for him*,
he sent the Holy Spirit."

4. *L'Esprit des Lois*, XXIV, 3.

5. Verse 51 deserves two observations. The "mysterious thing" Paul
"announces" is not that all will die but that "we will all be transformed,"
and this holds true "even if we will not all die." This hypothesis takes into
account those who might consider the Parousia as imminent, and who
could raise the question: "If the Parousia finds us still alive, how can we
be raised up without first passing through death?" That question faces
up to the difficulty that Paul speaks of in this passage about "being transformed," and not, as we might expect, about "being raised." In verse 52
he makes a good distinction: "The dead will be raised and we will be
transformed." Identifying himself with those who will see the Parousia,
Paul says "we," exactly as he had done earlier: "We who live, who
survive until his coming, will in no way have an advantage over those who
have fallen asleep" (1 Thes 4:15). This difficult statement has been
judiciously omitted in reading 25. Because it deals with a point that is
hardly of interest to our listeners, we have omitted it in our commentary.

In the preconciliar liturgy, on the other hand, the All Saints' Day
Mass and at clergy funerals the Vulgate translation, which states exactly
the opposite of the much more certain text that is adopted here: "We will
all be raised up, but we will not all be transformed." Fr. Allo says that this
translation had intended "to safeguard both the general resurrection and
the fact that all will not be 'changed,' because the damned will be there."
This "does not agree at all with the context in which there has been and
will be consideration only of the elect" (from Allo's commentary on this
passage in 1 Cor in the "Etudes Bibliques" collection).

6. Here we develop a word that has been correctly evaluated in the
New Testament text of the *Traduction Oecumenique de la Bible* (*TOB*): "For
as we know, if our earthly dwelling, *which is a tent*, is destroyed. . . . " The
lectionary does not retain that word, because σκενή (tent) signified
"body" when compared to a tent. The comparison recognizes the transitory character of human life. 2 Peter 1:13, 14 uses σκένωμα (a period of
time spent in a tent) to designate our life on earth. Wisdom 9:15 calls our
body γηωδες σκένος, an earthen or clay tent. "The earthen shelter weighs

down the mind that has many concerns." The comparison with death is explicit in Isaiah 38:12 (Ezechias' Canticle): "My dwelling, like a shepherd's tent, is struck down and borne away."

7. For better or for worse, we have used the words "expatriate" and "repatriate" in order to pair off the words which St. Paul contrasts three times in this passage: εκδεμεσαι (to be snatched away from one's country, to be exiled) and ενδεμεσαι (to have a domicile, to dwell in one's own country).

8. Cited by François Mauriac in *Blaise Pascal et sa soeur Jacqueline*, chap. XIV. Mauriac does not cite his source, and I have not been able to find the quote, or the exact reference, from M. Singlin.

9. If it would be advantageous to say more about the Apocalypse, which is such a poorly understood book, one may wish to use the presentation in the first and second part of the preceding commentary.

10. On the theme "God with" and the promise "I will be their God and they shall be my people," see Lv 26:11–12, Dt. 31:8, Ps 45/46:8, Jer 31:22, 33, Ez 37:26–27. Concerning Jesus' promise to "be with," see Mt 28:20, Mk 3:14, Lk 15:31 and 23:43, and Rv 3:20, 21.

GOSPELS

101. The True Values of the Christian Life

(*Mt 5: 1–12a*)

In the Light of the Beatitudes

Whenever one of our loved ones disappears from earth, we are deeply saddened by the loss we feel. We are inclined to reflect upon the life that has just ended. In some of our deceased sisters and brothers, we admire and perhaps envy their success in human, family, and professional endeavors. Their lives would have continued to flourish were it not for death's brutal interruption. In others, we detect a modest existence that had no great external influence and no sparkling relationships. In the lives of still other people, we seem to discern a series of failures and deceptions, the last of which is death.

That is a human and legitimate way of judging. But on this occasion we have come together in Christ Jesus, and we have just heard his word for our instruction and comfort.

The Beatitudes introduce Jesus' Sermon on the Mount. The lectionary reading has nothing directly to do with death; indeed, the same reading is used in the wedding liturgy, when the Beatitudes present a program of Christian happiness desired by the newlyweds. In today's funeral liturgy, the reading seems to be a light—in retrospect—by which to evaluate a terminated life, according to the value system Christ wished to teach us.

And so the reading brings us hope and comfort in our grief. Unlike the situation of marriage, there is no longer a question of viewing happiness, here below, in a household that begins new life. Now we are dealing with the happiness of living in heaven. Life in heaven is not only new, it is made new again: a life that lasts forever.

When Christ repeats the word *blest*, nine times in succession, he doesn't mean any achievement whatsoever, or a passing opportunity. Christ means full happiness, the kind to which every person deeply aspires. *Blest*, on this occasion, reminds us of "beatitude," which for the believer consists in the completely satisfying vision of God, in directly sharing in God's lasting and perfect happiness.

We can say the same thing about all the beatitudes: they are given in a sense that goes contrary to our expectations, whereas we would readily say: "Blest are the ambitious, blest are the strong, blest are the capable, blest are those who plan ahead . . . " That is completely different from Jesus' message.

The Poor, the Meek, Those Who Weep

The First Beatitude, which in a way contains all the rest, is perhaps the most disconcerting: *How blest are the poor in spirit*. It doesn't deal with those deprived of money, or even with those who are wealthy but don't know that they are slaves to their wealth.

The Beatitudes deal with that deep, interior poverty by which a person presents himself (or herself) before God as a stripped, disarmed being, who has confidence in God, not in oneself.

People who are humble before God are also humble before their brothers and sisters. *The poor in spirit* are indeed the same as the meek and *lowly*. By not seeking to dominate, humiliate, or exploit others, *they shall inherit the land* promised by God to those who keep his covenant, which is a covenant of love. Like Jesus, they live not to be served but to serve.

The Second Beatitude is the most astonishing—it even appears to contain a contradiction: *Blest are the sorrowing*. To resolve the apparent contradiction, some commentators have supposed that Jesus is describing converts who weep because of their sins. Other commentators suggest that the beatitude concerns those who suffer because of worldwide disorder, or the rarity of belief, etc. Such interpretations can be admitted; but this beatitude would then be identical with a subsequent beatitude, which concerns those who hunger and thirst for justice.

No—we must take Christ's statement as it stands. Besides, the beatitude directly refers to us today, who are mourning someone who has departed. Human life does not pass without mourning, without failures, without deceptions, without loneliness. Therefore tears are part of our lives. But if these tears are without bitterness, without rebellion, without self-pity and selfishness, *the sorrowing* will *be consoled*. This is not to be taken lightly, in the sense that these people will be humanly consoled or will always find someone to console them. Experience shows that this often happens, but not in every situation. According to the biblical and Gospel way of speaking, we must understand that *they shall be consoled* by God.

God himself said it on many occasions. In the Old Testament: "As a mother comforts her son, so will I comfort you" (Is 66:13). Jesus tells us in the Gospel: "Come to me, all you who are weary and find life burdensome, and I will refresh you" (Mt 11:28, reading 102). Finally, the Book of Revelation quotes Isaiah (25:8, see reading 7) and reveals the secrets of the last days: "God shall dwell with them and they shall be his people and he shall be their God who is always with them. He shall wipe every tear from their eyes, and there shall be no more mourning, crying out, or pain" (Rv 21:3–4, reading 33).

If one day this must be true for everyone, it is true, here and now, for the poor of heart and the meek, who carry their affliction, because such people have their heart open and disposed to God's tenderness.

The Merciful, Those Who Hunger for Justice, and the Peacemakers

The next beatitudes are easier to understand. They do not describe an apparently passive attitude but, rather, efficacious activity in the service of God's kingdom and one's neighbor.

Blest are they who hunger and thirst for holiness—that is, those who have an ardent desire for perfection in their relationship with God and with people. *They shall have their fill*, for they will be heard far beyond their wishes, because they will find unblemished justice and holiness in God.

Blest are the peacemakers—those who are not content with being easily appeased, who are never threatening and self-centered but who work to build peace, to reconcile people with God and with each other.

In fact, all the beatitudes can be understood only in reference to God. When we "laicize" the beatitudes, we empty them of their meaning. But that does not mean that some unbelievers do not practice the beatitudes better than some Christians. Even when their conscious goal is purely human, *the peacemakers* work in God's Spirit, as God said through the prophet Jeremiah: "I know well the plans I have in mind for you, plans for your welfare, not for woe! Plans to give you a future full of hope" (Jer 29:11).

The Persecuted

Those who work to build peace and those who hunger for justice face contradictions. They must battle those who wish to start war and perpetuate injustice. That is why the Eighth (and last) Beatitude is that of "the humbled and oppressed" (to borrow Dostoyevsky's title).[1] At the time when our Gospel of Matthew was redacted, this beatitude envisioned continuous persecution against Christ's apostles, which could end in death. Though not always to such an extreme, it is practically inevitable that, in the paradox of the Beatitudes, fidelity to Christ's ideal will trigger hatred and contradiction.

Pure Hearts

Now we must meditate on a beatitude which is especially important for our full understanding, because it can shed light on all the others. *Blest are the single hearted, for they shall see God.* We would be in error if we translate the words "heart" and "pure" in a modern, moralizing sense. For us, the heart is the center of affectivity, and purity is opposed to what is called the sin of the flesh. In that sense, "the pure of heart" would be Christians who are irreproachable sexually. Only perfectly chaste people would be able to *see God*, which would be nonsense. Jesus showed a predilection for sinners, and said to the Pharisees, who were "pure" by profession: "Let me make it clear that tax collectors and prostitutes are entering the kingdom of God before you," because they listened to John the Baptist, who preached conversion to them (Mt 21:31–32).

Contrary to our way of thinking, in Old Testament language the heart is not the organ of affectivity, or the organ of passionate love. The heart is the center of our thoughts, our reflections, our memory, which mulls over the past, and our will, which prepares for the future.

Single hearted refers to right intentions and loyal wills. We can think of Christians who have committed many mistakes throughout their lives but have been able to keep their hearts pure in this regard. Despite their blemishes, they have maintained their fundamental orientation toward God. In classical terminology, they have "retained charity," or at least a desire to love God with all their might, though that desire was weak at times. And their "conversion," which is always needed, consists in rediscovering and liberating that profound intention.

We can compare a "pure" or "single" heart to the "simple eye" about which our Lord spoke: "If your eyes are good, your body will be filled with light" (Mt 6:22).

Whenever Jesus opposed the Pharisees and treated them as hypocrites, it was because their deepest intention was too rigidly fixed on their own perfection, their own merits, instead of God. For that reason Jesus called them "blind" and "blind leaders of the blind" (Mt 15:14, 23:16–24; see Jn 9:40–41). Their hearts were not pure, their eyes were not simple, because their intention was not right.

But those whose intention is right will be "filled with light" (Mt 6:22): *They shall see God*, when God himself will complete their perfection. We hope, and we must pray, for that purification to be achieved soon.

A Hope for Today

Finally, we ask ourselves: "When will the hope that fills all the beatitudes be realized?"

The first reply must be that the hope is already realized. Jesus speaks of the present. When he says, over and over again, *blest*, he doesn't mean that we will be happy, or even that he wishes that we will be happy. He doesn't make promises, predictions, or wishes; he makes statements and declarations. *Blest* really means "You *are* happy."[2]

When Jesus said that, he was speaking to *his disciples*, who *gathered around him*. They were his contemporaries, living people, seated in the meadow *around him*.

It is surprising that he called them the *single hearted*, the *lowly*, and the *sorrowing*. Such statements, however, are explained in the reward itself. Here on earth, the reward is described in two beatitudes: *The reign of God is theirs*.[3]

As yet, "God's reign" is not heaven or the future life. It means belonging to Jesus Christ's kingdom, which begins here below, with faith and the practice of the Gospel. Jesus reveals to those who wish to follow him that the reign is already at their door.[4] Isn't this joyful news, and a powerful motive to be comforted, for *the single hearted* and *those persecuted for holiness' sake*?

The other beatitudes are rewarded with a future promise: *They shall inherit the land . . . they shall be consoled . . . they have their fill . . . mercy shall be theirs . . . they shall be called sons of God.* This will be realized in the next world.

What gives these everyday words an extraordinary charge of happiness and glory is that it will all be God's work. God will give himself fully to his sons and daughters in all the promises. The greatest promise is reserved for *the single hearted: they shall see God*, face to face. They will be absolutely satiated by the view, or, to put it more accurately, by contact with God's beauty, love, and infinite happiness. That will be the *great reward*.

Don't let that phrase trick us. We should not think of a payment, or bonus, or distribution of prizes and medals. The recompense will be nothing like that; it will be God himself. God gives us all the "beatitudes" here on earth, but in the obscurity of faith. Only when we go beyond the frontiers of this life will God fully give himself to us. Only then will we discover in the gift, which God had begun in silence and in the obscurity of our mediocrity, how precarious our earthly existence is.

This lesson should diminish our suffering by helping us to hope and ask for happiness—beatitude—for the deceased person whom we are mourning. That same lesson should also strengthen us who walk along the same road.

102. "Come to Me, All You Who Are Weary"

(*Mt 11:25–28*)

The final words of this Gospel passage are especially addressed to us, because we are mourning: *Come to me, all you who are weary and find life burdensome, and I will refresh you.* The burden we carry is the human condition, with death as its destiny. Our burden is an existence that may seem absurd to us, because it ends with a disappearance that looks like annihilation. A cruel and senseless separation is imposed on those who remain here on earth.

Can we be *refreshed* when we face the anguish that life inspires, when we face the death that ends life? What the Father wished to reveal to us through Jesus' words is the mystery of life, the true meaning of life. That's what Jesus came to show us, provided we are little children, *the merest children*. Why? Because this revelation remains *hidden from the learned and the clever*, who rely solely on their own experience, their knowledge, their wisdom—today we call it their "philosophy"—and are unable to heed the revelation of the kingdom Jesus came to bring us.

By contrast, *the merest children* are the poor, the humble, and the meek of the Beatitudes. Nothing prevents them from being wise and learned as well, but their wisdom and knowledge do not blind them to the Father's revelation, delivered by Jesus—the revelation guarded, deepened, and propagated by the Church. For science and philosophy can be highly intellectual and competent on the hunan level and, at the same time, terribly myopic—if not blind—with regard to the questions about the meaning of life and death, which arise in our experience.

We cannot find this meaning by becoming proud and confronting God himself, who knows and governs the world he created. Certainly none of us, by our own powers, can arrive at God's secrets. But the Father sent his Son among us to announce the mysteries of God's kingdom in human language, a language that Jesus, our brother, shares.

The essence of the mystery is that God thinks of us, is interested in us, and loves us. And the proof that God loves us is that he sent his Son to save us, who saved us by dying and rising for us. Thus he gave meaning to our death, of which his death is the prototype: a passage to God.

Therefore death is not the destruction of life, nor the negation of life. Death is life's crown and fulfillment. All of us will "find ourselves" in the Father's house.

That is what Jesus came to reveal to those who are child-like enough, that is, to those humble and open enough to receive. He claimed his capacity to reveal to us the mysteries of the kingdom: "The Father loves the Son," Jesus said, "and everything the Father does he shows him. . . . I solemnly assure you, the man who hears my word and has faith in him who sent me possesses eternal life" (Jn 5: 20, 24, reading 114).

Because Jesus *knows the Father* and enjoys full, loving intimacy with the Father, he *wishes to reveal to us* that God is not an indifferent potentate, but a true Father. God considers us to be his children. He wants only what's good for us, just as a human father does. He wants us to live forever with him and to share in his happiness, which Jesus called "eternal life." Isn't that all a father wants for his children?

Father, it is true. You have graciously willed it so. And being the all-powerful Father, he does whatever he wishes.

That is what Jesus *wishes to reveal to us.* He reminds us of it today, on the occasion of the departure of a member of our community. Jesus has shared our sorrow. He wept when his friend Lazarus died (reading 119). He now comes to *refresh* us with hope and trust.

103. Too Late!

(Mt 25:1 13)

The parable of the ten maidens is taken from an important section in St. Matthew's gospel. Chapters 24 and 25 group Jesus' teaching on the end of the world and the coming of the Son of Man. Because we read this parable on the occasion of a funeral, we will consider it as enlightening us concerning the death of each of us and the judgment that will follow immediately after our death. For the moment, we will not concentrate on the end of the world and the judgment of all humankind. In fact, before the Son of Man judges everyone and puts an end to human history, each of us will go to welcome him at that moment when our own history will end in death.

As a whole, these discourses, given by Jesus, concern the Last Judgment, but the different parables stress the conduct and responsibility of the individual: the faithful and watchful servant, contrasted with the wicked servant who profits from his master's delay by beating his companions and giving himself over to drunken living (24:45–51); the ten bridesmaids, some of whom have foresight while others are foolish (25:1–13); the three servants to whom the master confided talents, to be made fruitful as they await the master's return, but one of whom lacked confidence and initiative (25:14–30); and finally the Last Judgment itself, in which people will be divided on the Master's left and right, according to each one's conduct (25:31–46, reading 104, which follows this reading).

The beginning of the great discourse (24:1–44) warns all humanity, and the entire Church, to take it on themselves to be ready for the return of the Son of Man. The date is unknown, and may happen at any moment. Therefore everyone must be "watchful" and "ready" (24:43–44). The following parables, however, contain invitations to personal, prudent, and attentive vigilance to await the Lord, who will come for each "when the servant is not ready and least expects him" (24:50).

We should note that the parable of the ten young maidens ends with a word of warning to the foolish maidens: *I tell you, I do not know you.* But the parable's picture of this decisive hour has nothing funereal about it. It's a feast, a wedding, with a procession of lights that lead to a wedding-banquet hall. The Lord Jesus is presented to us as the groom (see Rv 19:9, 21:2, 9), for whom the bridesmaids wait impatiently. His arrival sets off a joyous noise: *The groom is here! Come out and greet him!*

The parable concludes with the stern warning: *Keep your eyes open, for you know not the day or the hour.* But this is not a criticism of the young women who are asleep, because *they all began to nod, then to fall asleep.* We have good reason to interpret the sleep of all the maidens as representing death, from which no creature can escape.

It was beforehand that they had to be watchful. The prudent young maids are those who made provision for oil for their torches before they went to sleep, in order to be ready to light his way when the bridegroom arrived. For the others, it was too late. Too late to share the oil of the prudent maidens and too late to *go to the dealers,* because *while they went off to buy it the groom arrived.*

The parable therefore illustrates a truth of primary importance: As long as we are alive, as long as we walk this journey, we can decide our final destiny. We can change directions, which is the same as saying we can be "converted." We can enter into eternal life, even here on earth, because this life consists in "knowing the true God, and the one God has sent, Jesus Christ" (Jn 17:3). As long as we are alive on earth, we can progress in the divine life that Jesus has given us and thus bear fruit, "fruit that must endure" (Jn 15:16) for all eternity.

As long as we are alive in this world, that is our preroga-
tive. But later, it will be too late. Lost time will not be re-
covered. We will be fixed forever in the state in which death
will surprise us. Perhaps the very moment of death will make
us take into account our real values, and at that supreme
moment we will be able to make a good choice. Who knows?

But let's not count on that chance. Life on earth was
given to us to acquire eternal life, and is not a mere interval
between life and death.

Therefore we must not allow ourselves to be surprised
by "the hour of our death," which may be unexpected. But
this doesn't mean we must always have our eyes fixed on the
grave, though Christians in past centuries have too often
made "preparation for death" a macabre, unhealthy exercise. God does not ask us to begin to "live our death" from
this moment on; that would mean living in desolation, with
an unreal outlook. God asks us to live the life he has given us.

We must not allow ourselves to be distracted or com-
promised by material pleasures, by the monotony or apparent mediocrity of our existence. We must courageously
perform according to our state in life. That is our task as a
citizen of this earth. We must be attentive to God and seek
his face with a prayerful and quiet faith; we must hear his
word; we must love our sisters and brothers as he has
loved us.

When we act in this manner, we do not allow ourselves
to be surprised by the shout, that joyful shout: *The groom is
here! Come out and greet him!*

104. "You Did It to Me"
(*Mt 25:31–46*)

We have just heard St. Matthew's description of the
Last Judgment, a description unequaled in all of Sacred

Scripture. Its vastness and majesty are extraordinary.

We are especially interested in the judgment account because we have come together to pray for one of our deceased brothers, and because the thought of death immediately raises the agonizing question: "How will God judge our brother, whom he has called to himself? What will be his eternal destiny?"

A staggering question! Our thoughts go to certain statements Jesus made, such as: "Whoever acknowledges me before men I will acknowledge before my Father in heaven. Whoever disowns me before men I will disown before my Father in heaven" (Mt 10:32–33 and parallel texts). Therefore, to be saved we must know and confess Christ explicitly.

But what about people who have not known and confessed him by a fully Christian belief and a fully Christian profession of faith? What about people who have not given complete and constant obedience to Christ's precepts and the precepts of his Church? Are they lost? What will happen to those who, perhaps, through no fault of their own, have not believed and have not realized the Christian ideal? To pose an even more radical question: "What are the chances for salvation for pagans and unbelievers?"

St. Paul tells us that when "God will judge through Jesus Christ the hidden comportment of men," he will take into account that pagans have obeyed God's law, which they did not recognize as such, when they fulfilled the work desired by the law that was "written in their hearts," that is, in "their conscience" (see Rom 2:14–16).

But in the judgment narrative by St. Matthew, Jesus offers an even clearer, more comforting teaching. He refers not only to the judgment of mediocre or fervent Christians. *All the nations will be assembled before him. All the nations*—that is, everyone: Jews and non-Jews, Christians and non-Christians.

Then *the king*, who is also the *Son of Man*, the Christ, will act as a *shepherd* (we recognize him as the one who said in Jn 10:11: "I am the good shepherd, the true shepherd"). *He will separate them into two groups, as a shepherd separates sheep from goats. The sheep he will place on his right hand, the goats on his left.*

The picture is clear. The white sheep, those who *have the Father's blessing*, are placed on his right side; the black goats, those *condemned*, are placed on his left.[5]

The division between the blessed and the damned is impressive; but an important observation should be made. Those who *have my Father' blessing*, Jesus says, *inherit the kingdom prepared for* them *from the creation of the world*. God wants what he has *prepared* for humankind, namely, the kingdom. In fact, God wishes all men and women to be saved (see 1 Tm 2:4).

The *everlasting fire prepared for the devil and his angels* is for those who profoundly and obstinantly have refused the salvation God offers. *Eternal fire* (which God did not prepare for human beings) will be the punishment of those who have chosen to associate themselves with the Demon and his angels.

What can we expect from the Judgment? *The king will say to those on his right: Come. You have my Father's blessing . . . for I was hungry and you gave me food . . . I was a stranger and you welcomed me . . . I was in prison and you came to visit me.*

Jesus often said that everything we give to the least of his disciples is given to Him: "Whoever welcomes a child such as this for my sake welcomes me. . . . Whoever gives you a drink of water because you belong to Christ will not go without his reward" (Mk 9:37, 41, and parallel passages).

At the "particular" or individual judgment, those whom Christ blesses because of their good deeds are dumbfounded. They may not have fed, clothed, and visited the poor in Christ's name. He wasn't even in their thoughts! Many of them may never have heard of him: *Lord, when did we see you?* But Jesus reveals to them the close bond that unites him to all misfortunates, whom he calls "my brothers": *As often as you did it for one of my least brothers, you did it to me.*[6]

Note the repetition of the word "did." The same word is used in the sentencing of the damned: *As often as you neglected to do it to one of these least ones, you neglected to do it to me.* The condemnation is motivated not by great crimes, but by a general omission. Likewise, in the parable about Lazarus and the rich man, we are not told the rich man was plunged in the "flame" for having committed injustices but for having *seen* the poor man about to die at his doorstep.

Beautiful thoughts, beautiful words, beautiful professions of faith will have less import: "None of those who cry out, 'Lord, Lord,' will enter the kingdom of God but only the one who does the will of my Father in heaven" (Mt 7:21).

Among the people of *all the nations*, *assembled* before *the royal throne*, will be Christians. They will be judged not on their personal witness, or acts of piety, but on their conduct toward the *least brothers*, who are their brothers and sisters and, especially, are Jesus' brothers and sisters.

As our gospel shows us, there will be many surprises, of one kind or other, on Judgment Day!

What is the close bond, the fraternity, the quasi identity (*you did it to me*) between Jesus and the poor?

We find a basis in the fact that Jesus lived as a poor person, having been born with a manger for his crib and working thirty years as a village craftsman. In his life as a wandering preacher, he had no place to lay his head (see Mt 8:20), and he helped the poor by doing good deeds (see Lk 8:3).

The much deeper and more profound basis is that God's Son was stripped of all his divine privileges in order to take on the condition of a slave, obedient even in death on the cross, the punishment reserved for slaves (Phil 2:7–8): "though he was rich" as God, "he made himself poor" (2 Cor 8:9).

Finally, Jesus considered as basic to his mission the bringing of the kingdom to the poor (Lk 4:18, Mt 11:5), and he proclaimed that the kingdom belongs to the poor, who for that reason are blessed (Lk 6:20 and parallel passages).

Therefore, it is not surprising that Jesus called the poor *my brothers*, and that he considered what was done for them as done for himself.

Furthermore, we note, St. Matthew placed this surprising Last Judgment narrative immediately before the beginning of the passion account, in which Jesus shows himself to be poor and abandoned among all the poor.

May Jesus' teaching give us great hope. Despite the faults and omissions in faith and religion that our departed friend may be guilty of, Christ's definitive judgment considers what the deceased did for little ones and the poor as having been done for Jesus himself.

When the deceased acted in this way, did he know he was helping Christ in person? Perhaps. At any rate, he fulfilled the essence of Christ's law: "Such as my love has been for you, so must your love be for each other. This is how all will know you for my disciples: your love for one another" (Jn 13:34–35).

"Let us love in deed and truth and not merely talk about it" (1 Jn 3:18).

105. The Reward for Self-Denial
(*Mk 10:28–30*)

There are people whose lives seem lonely, poor, and stripped of worldly possessions—so they appear to us. But their death reveals to us that they were (and are) magnificently rich in God's eyes, which is all that really matters.

Jesus has just invited a rich young man to follow him, but the rich man would not make that decision. He determined to keep his wealth. And Jesus made this comment about the man's failure to follow him: "How hard it is for the rich to enter the kingdom of God!" (Mk 10:23).

Then Peter asked about his own situation and that of the other apostles, *who have put aside everything to follow you*. Jesus replied by affirming that such a sacrifice would merit a magnificent reward.[7] Nevertheless, we should examine some important aspects of Jesus' statement, because careless interpretation might give a completely distorted meaning to what Jesus said.

First of all, Jesus spoke of "reward"; but this word, in its ordinary sense, is not compatible with the Gospel as a whole. Therefore we should not imagine that those who "put everything aside" did so with a view of being rewarded. If that were the case, their renouncement would be only apparent and no more than a disguised form of selfishness. Surely, they didn't *put aside everything* because they hated human nature and were disgusted with life. A purely negative renouncement has no value.

Jesus said: those who *have put aside everything to follow* him.

Self-denial, therefore, has worth only if it is inspired by love. Remember the calling of the first apostles, who fished the Lake of Tiberias: "Jesus called them, and immediately they abandoned boat and father to follow him" (Mt 4:22, Lk 5:11). That's what St. Peter meant when he said: *We have put aside everything to follow you.*

The apostles did not "put everything aside" just because of Jesus' personality and doctrine, which were so attractive and appealing. Such renouncement would still be inspired by selfishness and desire for a harmonious life. Jesus says in our reading: "and because of *the gospel*." ("Gospel" signifies preaching and mission rather than a book or a doctrine.)

The total renouncement that Jesus rewards is inspired by fraternal charity, by the desire to imitate Jesus and to continue his mission of bringing the kingdom's Good News to the poor and to all people. St. Paul describes his own apostolate in the same way: "We are seen to be poor, yet we enrich many. We seem to have nothing, yet everything is ours!" (2 Cor 6:10).

Jesus promises neither an unusual reward for renouncement nor an indemnity that would repay what was lost. Renouncement is really wealth. Indeed, possession of material wealth closes people in on themselves and makes them isolated, sterile, and "poor" individuals. But those who are detached from their riches and from their selfishness, in self-sacrifice for a higher cause, are open to a higher life, shared with all humankind. Such people are truly rich.

This is the meaning of the mysterious *hundred times* that Jesus spoke about. Freedom and fraternity, brought about by the renouncement of selfish possessions, bring an even richer possession, which can be shared. That is what we learn from the description of the first Christian community in the Acts of the Apostles: "The community of believers were of one heart and one mind. . . . There was no one needy among them, for all who owned property or houses sold them. . . . They used to lay their goods at the feet of the apostles to be distributed to everyone according to his need" (Acts 4:32, 34, 35).

But let us not imagine that those who renounced their properties obtained security and comfort in exchange, analogous to what they renounced. After enumerating all the riches that are lost and found again—*homes, brothers and sisters, mothers, children and property*—our Lord adds a bitter phrase: *and persecution.*

Christ's disciple will always be persecuted, as he was. Jesus had warned his apostles about that: "No slave is greater than his master. They will harry you as they harried me" (Jn 15:20). He also gives the reason for the persecution: "The reason the world hates you is that you do not belong to the world" (Jn 15:19).

When people leave everything for the sake of Jesus and the Gospel, they defy the world, which is animated by selfishness and vain desire. Therefore Jesus does not tell us that his apostles possess on this earth—or, as he says, *in this present age*—the nicest and most agreeable life. He merely tells us (and this is already happening *in this present age*): Life is much less bare and desolate than it may appear in the world's estimation. This allows us to admire, and even envy, the lives of many people whom otherwise we might pity.

Death puts an end to a life of renouncement and sacrifice. Death brings us into *the age to come*—which does not mean into dwelling places for sisters and brothers. *The age to come* means being alive with God, in heaven, and possessing God's infinite riches and happiness.

106. Jesus' Prayer before His Death

(Mk 14:32–36)

When death confronts us with its horror and sadness, we should recall that Jesus, too, was confronted in the same way—though he is "the Author of life" (Acts 3:15), the One in whom "life is found" (Jn 1:4), the One who has "life because of the Father" (Jn 6:57) and "is life" in person (Jn 14:6). Jesus was certain that he would be raised from the dead, and yet, when he encountered death, he became *filled with fear and distress*.

How can it surprise us that we, who are weak and

wretched, become fearful and anxious when *we* face death? But Jesus serves as our model because he wished to become "like his brothers in every way." "He himself was tested through what he suffered and is able to help those who are tempted" (Heb 2:17–18).

On Holy Thursday evening, we find Jesus with his disciples at *a place named Gethsemane*. Because he went there frequently, he foresaw that Judas would know where to find him in order to have him arrested and led to the cross (see Jn 18:2).

He said to his disciples: Sit down here while I pray. He needed to be alone for his prayer (see Mk 1:35, Mt 14:23), but *he took along with him Peter, James and John*, his intimate friends. Jesus had taken them to Jairus' house, to give them the opportunity to assist in his victory over death (Mk 5:22); he had led them up the mountain, on which he was transfigured, to show them his future glory (Mk 9:2 and parallel texts). They should have been able to support him in the assault of his approaching death. But no. Every man and woman dies alone, absolutely alone.

Jesus told them: *My heart is filled with sorrow to the point of death.* He experienced the sadness that only imminent death can produce. He repeated the exhortation he so often addressed to them (Mt 24:42, Mk 13:35, etc.): *Stay awake.* Not merely to remain watchful, but to be spiritually attentive in habitual prayer. It is our duty, too, whenever someone we love approaches death, to watch and pray with and for that person. But unfortunately, we often excuse ourselves from such fraternal assistance. Didn't Peter, James, and John— Jesus' closest disciples—fall asleep at Gethsemane?

So Jesus was alone, and his prayer was an intense supplication. *He fell to the ground, praying.* He asked *that if it were possible this hour might pass him by.* The "hour" Jesus referred to was not the present hour but the approaching, imminent, unavoidable hour of his trial and execution.

I mentioned earlier that Jesus was alone, and that each of us is inevitably alone, at the hour of death. That's true, humanly speaking, but it's not true on God's side. God never leaves us alone.

A few moments earlier, Jesus had said to his disciples: "An hour is coming—has indeed already come—when you will be scattered and each will go his own way, leaving me alone. (Yet I can never be alone; the Father is with me)" (Jn 16:32).

Death is our most immediate encounter with God, an encounter that would be terrifying if we were not inclined to pray. Therefore Jesus prayed to his Father.

He addressed him with the most tender word, *Abba*, which means *O Father*. But this word, in Jesus' native language, was the word small children used when they spoke to "Daddy."[8] It's the same word that begins the prayer Jesus taught to his disciples. And at this important hour, he used the prayer himself. He began his petition as we do in the Mass prayers, when we recall that God is all powerful: *Father, you have the power to do all things.* Then he made his request explicit: *Take this cup away from me.*

The "cup," the chalice, represents sacrifice. It is filled not only with bitter "liquid"—suffering and death, which Jesus must drink willingly but also with love. This is how suffering becomes a meritorious and redemptive sacrifice, and Jesus was well aware of this fact. At the Last Supper he had offered and shared the "cup of the new covenant," and he commanded his disciples to offer and share it "in his memory."

But Jesus was as human as we are. His first human reaction was to flee from death, and to deny it. However, to submit his human will to the divine will, he prayed: *But let it be as you would have it, not as I.*

Then Jesus was comforted and reassured. He regained his composure through his prayer. The Father did not grant

his spontaneous request, but gave him the strength to accomplish his mission fully, to face "his hour."

Calmly, with dignity, he had received the traitor and
the soldiers who had arrested him. He had prevented his
disciples from defending him; and even told them: "Am I
not to drink the cup the Father has given me?" (Jn 18:11).

Faced with our own death and with the death of our
loved one, we have one resource: prayer. That's what Jesus
taught us at Gethsemane. We frequently say the Lord's
Prayer, but we say it mechanically. We must place our
entire, childlike obedience, our complete trust, in God, as
we repeat, as Jesus did: *Abba, Father* . . . may your will be
done on earth as it is in heaven, *but let it be as you would have it,
not as I.*

107. Jesus Died to Live Once Again

(*Mk 15:33–34a, 34c, 37–39, 16:1–6*)

Christians must not allow themselves to be depressed
and troubled by death—though death, certainly, is a fearsome reality. It is normal that we are afraid and saddened
by death. But our belief necessitates that we consider death
with serenity, because death is a part of what our faith
reveals to us: We have the certitude of being saved from sin
and death through the death of our model and Leader,
Jesus Christ.

That's why we attach a crucifix to the casket of our
dead. That's why the cross is so predominant on cemetery
graves. The cross is not a sign of sadness, but of hope. It
encourages us in our time of trial.

The reading we have just heard from St. Mark's gospel
reminds us of some characteristics of Jesus' death. At
Calvary, between noon and *midafternoon, darkness fell on the*

whole countryside, as if to proclaim the human death of him who is "the life" and "the light of the human race" (Jn 1:4). Jesus had described himself as "the light of the world" (Jn 8:12, 9:5, 12:46).

For a long time, Jesus agonized on the cross. Then suddenly he *cried out in a loud voice, my God, my God, why have you forsaken me?* Indeed, he had been betrayed, whipped, crowned with thorns, nailed to the wood of the cross, and pierced by a lance. His friends—with the exception of some women—abandoned him. And God himself, who could have helped him by a miracle (see Mt 26:53), apparently did nothing to deliver Jesus or to comfort him. It seems that Jesus also felt that he was abandoned by the Father.

Can we picture a deeper agony? Can we believe that God's Son, the beloved of the Father (see Mt 4:17 and parallel texts, 17:5 and parallel texts, Jn 3:35, etc.), submitted to agony, to the sense of being abandoned, which was as cruel as people experience who are most agonized by their own death?

Nevertheless, Jesus' outcry must not be interpreted as expressing real despair. Surely, it expressed genuine agony, but we must remember that his shout was a quotation that begins a psalm (21/22), which Jesus wished to recall in its entirety and which ends in a prayer of thanks giving for final victory.[9]

Then Jesus, uttering a loud cry, breathed his last. At that moment the curtain in the sanctuary was torn in two from top to bottom—a reference, surely, to Jesus' death that ended worship in the Jewish religion, as reserved for one people, in order to inaugurate a new faith that would be open to all men and women.

The centurion who stood guard over him . . . declared, "Clearly this man was the Son of God!" This pagan, Roman soldier did not proclaim our belief in Jesus' divinity, but he witnessed Jesus' innocence and holiness. Without knowing it, he was the first of many women and men who, despite Jesus' death (or rather *because* of his death), recognize Jesus as God's Son, as God himself, equal to his Father.

The dead Jesus was placed in the tomb, as we affirm in St. Paul's Creed (1 Cor 15:4) and in the Sunday Mass Creed. His death was not a pretense. He wished to share our human condition, even in its profoundest misery.

The women, however, did not forget him; but they could not go to venerate the tomb because of a stricture of the Sabbath, which began on the evening of the crucifixion. So they went to the tomb as early as possible, on the morning of *the first day of the week*, the "third day." They wished to offer Jesus burial honors by *anointing* his tortured body.

They saw that the entrance of the tomb, though formerly closed by *a huge stone*, was accessible. *They entered the tomb* (which according to Jewish custom was a room hewn in rock), where they expected to find their dear, dead Jesus. But *they saw a young man, dressed in a white robe*, who was surely an angel, one of the heavenly messengers whom God has sent to humankind. *This frightened them thoroughly*, which is normal in an encounter with a divine being.

But he reassured them: "You need not be amazed! You are looking for Jesus of Nazareth, the one who was crucified. He has been raised up; he is not here."

St. Luke also reports the angel's words, in an even more striking manner: "Why do you search for the Living One among the dead? He is not here; he has been raised up" (Lk 24:5–6).

Such an affirmation has historic interest, but it would not console us in our mourning if the passage concerned only Jesus. We know, however, that Jesus' resurrection is but the first in an immense procession: the procession of all people saved, who become one body with him.

The holy women of Easter morning went to the tomb in piety and sadness. To venerate a dead man. Their encounter with the angel must have troubled them, as did their discovery of the empty tomb. But their joy returned when they heard the wonderful word: *He has been raised up; he is not here.*

May this message also bring peace to our sad and troubled hearts, because we know, through St. Paul, that "if we have died with him we shall also live with him" (2 Tm 2:11).

108. "You Can Dismiss Your Servant in Peace"

(Lk 2:22b, 25–32)

Death is often painful and sometimes tragic, for the persons who die and for those who are present when death comes. Often, we see death as an uprooting, a failure or an injustice, especially when death comes early in life. On the other hand, there are gentle and peaceful deaths that seem to be the fulfillment and crown of a very full and productive life. That's how *some* old people die—such as Simeon, whom we've just heard described in the gospel.

In the Old Testament, the deaths of certain just people are presented as a completely natural event, following a long life ("filled with days"). This was true of Abraham (Gn 25:8), Isaac (Gn 35:9), David (1 Chr 29:28), and old Tobit, who "died peacefully" (Tb 14:1).

But Simeon cannot really be compared to those ancient patriarchs. He lived in a time when faithful Jews were enthusiastic in their hope for the Messiah. They awaited *the consolation of Israel,* God's liberation of their country from foreign occupation. *The Holy Spirit was upon him* means that

Simeon was one of the "Lord's poor," whose heart was entirely open and ready to receive divine enlightenment. *It was revealed to him by the Holy Spirit that he would not experience death until he had seen, with his own eyes, the Anointed of the Lord.* the Messiah, the One whom God had consecrated as Consoler and Savior (see Lk 2:11).

Inspired by the Spirit, he came to the temple. Certainly he went there often; but the Spirit urged him to go to the Temple on that day, the very moment *when the parents brought in the child Jesus,* whom they intended to present to God.

Jesus was an ordinary infant, quite like all other infants. He was brought by a young couple, who looked as ordinary as could be. Therefore the Holy Spirit's impulse was needed so that Simeon might *take the child in his arms and bless God* (he sang a song of thanksgiving) *in these words:* "*Now, Master, you can dismiss your servant in peace* (which means Simeon could die); *you have fulfilled your word.*"

Simeon did not fear death. He accepted and desired death because he saw that the Lord's promise was fulfilled. Enlightened by the Spirit, he prophesied that the tiny infant, who was silent and perhaps asleep, would conquer death through his own death. Simeon immediately prophesied the contradictions the *Anointed of the Lord* would encounter later on, which would lead him to the cross and result in the piercing of his mother's heart (see Lk 2:34–35).

Bossuet gives an excellent explanation of Simeon's words: "Now that I have seen the mediator who expiates sin by his death, I can depart in peace: in peace, because my Lord will conquer sin and will save those who believe; in peace, because death will soon be disarmed and will no longer be able to trouble those who have hope; in peace, because a God become victim will reconcile heaven and earth, and because the blood he is ready to shed will open the door of the holy places. There our eyes will discover him; there we will contemplate him in his glory; there we will see only him, because he will be all in all. He will illumine every spirit by his radiant face and will penetrate every heart by the qualities of his infinite goodness."[10]

We are not in the same situation as Simeon, who rejoiced to hold Jesus himself in his arms, the incarnate Word who came to our earth for a few years. But our faith and our hope, which are in continuity with Simeon's, are more precise and certain. We find the meaning in St. Peter's words to the early Christians, who, like us, believed without having seen (see Jn 20:29): "There is cause for rejoicing here. You may for a time have to suffer the distress of many trials . . . all that must lead to praise, glory, and honor when Jesus Christ appears. Although you have never seen him, you love him, and without seeing you now believe in him, and rejoice with inexpressible joy touched with glory because you are achieving faith's goal, your salvation" (1 Pt 1:6–9, reading 27).

Simeon held the infant Jesus in his arms—but only for an instant. And because he was filled with the Spirit, this was not a mere external contact. The Christian, however, possesses Jesus much more profoundly, through a faith that enables Jesus to live in our heart and through belonging to the Church, which is his Body. Therefore the Christian's hope is even more lively and certain than Simeon's: "Christ in you, your hope of glory" (Col 1:27).

Thus we understand how an elderly Christian can await death peacefully, and even welcome it with the Nunc Dimittis thanksgiving: *Now, Master, you can dismiss your servant in peace: you have fulfilled your word.*

As for us, we will pray that our friend will see, without delay, the *saving deed* and the *light* he awaited here on earth. Through the Mass, we will offer God *the Anointed of the Lord*, as he was offered by Mary and Joseph in the Temple. We will ask that Jesus, risen and victorious over death, may give all Christians faith and hope to look at death with less fear and more trust.

109. Jesus Raises an Only Son from the Dead

(Lk 7:11–17)

John the Baptist sent his disciples to ask Jesus: "Are you the One who must come, or should we look for another?" Jesus replied: "Go and report to John what you have seen and heard. The blind recover their sight, cripples walk, lepers are cured, the deaf hear, dead men are raised to life" (Lk 7:19, 22 = Mt 11:2–5).[11] By quoting the prophecies of Isaiah (35:5–6, 26:19, 61:1), Jesus wished to make known that he was indeed the awaited Messiah.

He said: "Dead men are raised to life," as though this had been a recurring miracle, but the Gospels report only three accounts of Jesus' raising people from the dead: Jairus' young daughter (Mt 9:18–25 and parallel texts), the son of the widow of Naim, and his friend Lazarus (Jn 11, readings 118 and 119). How, then, can we explain the Gospels' reticence, when the Acts of the Apostles tells of *two* resurrections, enacted by Peter (Tabitha: Acts 9:36–42) and by Paul (Eutychus: Acts 20:7–12)? Didn't their power come from Jesus (Mt 10:8)? The reason surely lies in the fact that such victories over death were incomplete and passing, because their beneficiaries were returned merely to earthly existence, which must one day come to an end. They were imperfect images of Jesus' definitive victory, his own resurrection.

In fact, God raised Jesus to bring his humanity to a glorious and divine life. "We know that Christ, once raised from the dead, will never die again; death has no more power over him" (Rom 6:9). Besides, the provisional resurrections were isolated, individual benefits. Christ's resurrection is our precedent of eternal life, which is happiness of body and soul, for all men and women who are saved.

Christ is "the firstborn of the dead" (Col 1:18), firstborn of those whom God "predestined to share the image of his Son, that the Son might be the firstborn of many brothers" (Rom 8:29).

Because death is thus the gateway into eternity and the necessary passage to a life of perfect happiness, shouldn't we consider death a desirable benefit? Isn't it wrong for a Christian to regard death as a sorrowful ordeal? Not really.

In our gospel, we are struck by Jesus' compassion when he confronted death and the distress that death inflicts on people. *Upon seeing* the poor *widowed mother*, who was taking her *only son*, her sole support, to the grave, Jesus *was moved with pity*. Literally St. Luke means that Jesus was emotionally and visibly shaken. The resurrection of Lazarus was not only a gesture to manifest the power of the *Lord*, conqueror of death, but also the expression of his mercy toward all the misfortunate.

In the very human pity of Jesus, in whom we can see his Father's face (see Jn 14:9, Heb 1:3), we learn that God "is human," that he has pity on us, and that he abhors death. "God did not make death," because "he does not rejoice in the destruction of the living" (Wis 1:13, 2:23). "It saddens the Lord to see his friends die" (Ps 115/116:15).[12] And thus we see Jesus weep at the death of his friend Lazarus (Jn 11:35–36, reading 119), and his intense agony at the approach of his own death (Mk 14:33–34, reading 106; Jn 12:27, reading 120).

Let us add that the *widowed mother* of an *only son* can be compared to the Church. Surely the Church has an immense multitude of children: all the baptized, and all the men, women, and children of every era. Moreover, every child is unique for the Church, because she knows the infinite price of a child's eternal happiness. She knows that Jesus would give his life for each one of them. Which is why the Church,

with prayers and intercession, accompanies the passing of her
children and consoles the survivors by proclaiming that God
does not want to see his friends held fast in the bonds of
death (see Ps 15/16:10).

110. "Keep Yourselves Ready"
(*Lk 12:35–38, 40*)

Watch—watch and pray; keep yourselves ready! Jesus
often repeated that kind of recommendation in the first
three gospels.[13]

In St. Matthew and St. Mark, the warnings are found
in the discourses on Jerusalem's destruction, which prefigures
the world's end and the coming of the Son of Man. Therefore Jesus' words, which are addressed to the entire Church
and the whole human race, concern a global and cosmic
event. But for those who will not be alive at that moment, the
warnings apply to the decisive encounter each of us experiences at the moment of death. St. Luke, however, has set
them in another context: an exhortation to be detached
from riches and to trust in Providence. And so the reading
we have just heard is quite appropriate for helping us meditate on our preparation for death.

Death is certain; but like the servants in our parable,
we do not know when it will occur. Their master will surely
return, but they do not know the hour. Therefore they must
always be ready.

But this doesn't mean that the servants must be, as it
were, hypnotized and paralyzed by waiting. Genuine
preparation for death doesn't consist in forgetting to be
alive! The warning, *let your belts be fastened around your waists
and your lamps be burning*, seems to exhort the servants not to
abandon their activity. In a very similar parable, St. Mark

says that the master, at his departure, "placed his servants in charge, each with his own task" (Mk 13:34).

The *fastened belts* and *burning lamps* have nothing to do with unconcern, or laziness, and even less with lugubrious inertia.[14]

Preparation for death does not consist in activity but in accomplishing one's duty, day after day, and in contributing as much as we can to the building of the earthly city and God's kingdom as well, especially by serving and loving our brothers and sisters. Surely we must be "watchful" and "ready" and, as several New Testament texts say, "sober" (see 1 Thes 5:6–8, Rom 13:13, 1 Pt 4:7, 5:8). This means that we should not be entirely absorbed in mundane work or distracted by the commodities and joys of our life here below. It also means that we should have a free and open spirit, so that we can hear God's word and its precautions.

Among the precautions, we must take death into account, which makes its presence felt with the infirmities and sicknesses of relatives and friends. In a very personal and urgent manner, our Lord repeated his exhortations to vigilance and prayer to the three disciples he brought with him to the Garden of Olives.[15] But they were not able to "stay awake even one hour with him" (Mt 26:40).

Indeed, it is expecially our Lord's death that interests us, instructs us, and nourishes our vigilance and our hope. Our commitment to live our baptism has consecrated us to die "in the Lord" and to live the Easter mystery. This happens not only every year at Easter but at every Sunday Mass, when we offer and share in the sacrifice of the dead and risen Christ. For one of Christ's faithful, the Mass is the most Christian and most efficacious way to prepare for death.

111. We Die with Jesus in Order to Be with Him in Paradise

(Lk 23:33–34, 39–46, 50, 52–53)

The narrative of Jesus' passion and death is eminently capable of making us envision, with humility and confidence, the mystery of death—our own death and the deaths of those we love.

The four evangelists left us four passion narratives that agree in their entirety and in the way the events unfold. In a sublime manner, St. John's text presents us with the Messiah as priest and king, who majestically celebrates the liturgy of his sacrifice. The closely related accounts of Mark and Matthew insist on the injustice and the mockeries that victimized Jesus, and we have just heard a section of St. Luke's account. With his usual emphasis, Luke describes our Savior (see Lk 2:11) and his mercy toward sinners, who are the most abandoned and the most despised people.

Jesus has been crucified, which means he was attached to the cross with nails through his hands and feet. An atrocious way of suffering! But instead of complaining and cursing his torturers, Jesus prayed for them: *Father, forgive them; they do not know what they are doing.*

The responsibility of the people who put God's Son to death was mitigated by their ignorance (see Acts 3:17, 1 Cor 2:8). And we know that Jesus was put to death not only by his actual executioners but by all sinners, ourselves included. Because the Son petitioned his Father, at the very moment he achieved our salvation, do we have any reason to think the Father is not ready to pardon sinners when they are at their hour of death?

As companions, the crucified Jesus had two *criminals*, who died with him, on his right and on his left. One of them *blasphemed him*, but the other recognized their guilt and

Jesus' innocence. Furthermore, he recognized Jesus as the Messiah, as the King who will *enter his reign* at the end of time. And in his agony the man asked: *Jesus, remember me.* Jesus forgave all the man's sins and answered his plea beyond his expections: "I assure you: *this day you will be with me in paradise.*"

For the forgiven man, as for Jesus, the hour of death was also the hour of glory (see Jn 12:23, 13:31, 17:1, 5). The evil man's death, which appears to be a fulfillment of defeat and punishment, is really a victory, A momentary but profound yearning redeemed a life of crime. By uniting himself to Jesus in death, he obtained the favor of never being separated from him. That very day he was in paradise, which we should not picture with childlike fantasies. The passage defines heaven in these words: "being with Jesus."

Jesus died with complete confidence and trust. He modified a psalm (30/31:6) that petitions the "Lord God of truth," the Lord God of faithfulness. With tenderness, Jesus addressed his Father as he told us to do when we repeat the filial prayer he taught us (Lk 11:2, see 23:34): *Father, into your hands I commend my spirit.*

The Church inserts the same request in the prayer of Compline, which it recommends to us in the evening when we are about to go to sleep—an image of death. May that prayer obtain for us the grace to enter death as into peaceful sleep!

112. "Stay with Us. Evening Is Near."

(*Lk 24:13–35* [*Long Form*])
(*Lk 24:13–26, 28–35* [*Short Form*])

When Jesus died on Calvary, his followers believed that everything had ended. Based on the Church's belief, we know that only his mother kept faith in him; but the Gospels

tell us nothing about that. The Gospels say that even the
faithful few, who remained at the foot of the cross, including
John, the "beloved disciple," did not believe in the resurrection (before they entered the empty tomb) (Jn 8:20).
Mary Magdalene contined to cry, even as she stood before
Jesus (Jn 20:2, 11). The holy women went to the tomb for
the purpose of enbalming a dead man (Mk 16:1).

St. Luke's gospel has shown us two disciples who were
overcome by sadness and confusion when they left Jerusalem.
Incognito, the risen Jesus joined them and questioned them,
and their response explains the cause of their distress. They
had pictured Jesus as a political liberator, whose power and
influence could be exercised only on this earth, in visible
fashion.

If they (and we) had remained on this temporal level,
it is evident that death is definitive failure, the end of every
hope. Some women claimed that Jesus was alive again. But
how could they admit the resurrection, which they imagined
as a resurrection of the former life?

Jesus himself *approached and began to walk with them. However, they were restrained from recognizing him.* How could they
see him, when they were unable to "tune into him" with
faith?

Let us see how Jesus consoled these wayfarers and accompanied them on their journey.

He interpreted for them every passage of the Scripture. He made
them understand that his death, which was neither an unforeseen accident nor a hopeless failure, was part of God's
providential plan.

*Did not the Messiah have to undergo all this so as to enter into
his glory?* Indeed, that's exactly what he did. We often find
that expression in the Gospels (see Mt 16:21 and parallel
texts, and Lk 17:25, 24:7, 44) and in Acts (1:16, 3:21).
In God's plan of love and salvation, Christ's death does not

signify a fatality but the bond established between Christ's humiliation and suffering and the glory he attained by saving all men and women in that manner. Thus Jesus' death, and consequently the death of his sisters and brothers, is not an end but a means.

The explanation that Jesus provided is not simply a theory. It enlightened his two companions and gave them courage. They understood that they had been victims of an illusion—that the Messiah's undertaking was not an escapade with no future. Soon they would say: *"Were not our hearts burning inside us as he talked to us on the road and explained the Scriptures to us?"*

As yet, they had not identified their traveling companion, but he brought them so much peace that they did not want him to leave: *"Stay with us. It is nearly evening."* And he enlightened them!

At table, Jesus blessed God and broke the bread, as he had done at the multiplication of the loaves and at the Last Supper, at which these two disciples had not been present. Now, enlightened by his words, they grasped the sign of sharing and love.

With that their eyes were opened and they recognized him. As a result, they believed that he was indeed risen, as they had been told. But because his resurrection had introduced Jesus into new life and because their faith no longer needed visible support, Jesus immediately *vanished from their sight.*

His disappearnace did not destroy their faith and enthusiasm, and they *returned to Jerusalem* to share their experience with the eleven apostles, who also had seen the Risen One.

We are not able to make an exact application of this story, which concerns Jesus' death and resurrection, to the death and resurrection of the friend we pray for today. Nevertheless, we can draw a comparison and learn a lesson from it.

Like the Emmaus disciples, we are overcome with grief if we see events only from an external, purely human perspective. The teachings of the faith help us understand, or at least sense, that the death of each of us is within God's plan and that, for every baptized Christian, death is the door to resurrection, just as death was for Christ, with whom we are united.

Rather than take pride in our sensitivity, which has been wounded, let us listen to Jesus, who travels with us. Let us ask him to warm our hearts once again, as we tell him: *Stay with us.*

We can sit down at his table and share his meal. For us, he is always invisible. But if we are believers, we recognize his presence with certitude when he takes bread, says the benediction, and breaks the bread and gives it to us. This is what Jesus will do at this Mass through the words and actions of the priest, who represents him.

Finally, we know that this sacrament of unity and friendship allows us to encounter in Christ, in a real but invisible way, the person who has just disappeared from our sight. "Because the loaf of bread is one, we the many" the — humanly living and the other living, whom we call the dead—are "one body, for we all partake of the one loaf" (1 Cor 10:17), the "bread of life" (Jn 6:48), the body of the risen Christ.

113. God So Loved the World

(*Jn 3:16–17*)

The very short gospel passage that we've just heard has much meaning! It begins by reminding us that God loves the world, that "God is love" (1 Jn 4:8). He created the world through love, to make his love radiant, and to give his creatures the chance to share in his life and happiness.

The world that has fallen into sin? Yes. This doesn't keep God from loving the world. In fact, he loves the world so much *that he gave his only Son*, his beloved Son.

God *gave* him to the world, which means he not only *sent the Son into the world*, through the incarnation, but he delivered him to death on the cross. Therefore, even the death of other people is not a loss, provided that death is accepted with belief in God's Son, who died for them.

Death opens into *eternal life*. This means that God gives himself in giving his Son, because *eternal life* is God himself, who gives himself to women and men in order to unite them to himself and to share his life with them.

Later on, Jesus will indeed judge. That's what we repeat each Sunday: Christ "will come to judge the living and the dead" in his second coming—his coming "in glory" at the end of time. But that's not why he came the first time, in humility, poverty, and mercy.

Under the "regime" of his first coming, under which we live, all men and women are called to be *saved*, provided they *believe in him*. May the death of those we mourn inspire us not so much with fear that they are judged, but with hope that they are *saved*, because *God so loved the world!*

114. Passing from Death to Life

(Jn 5:24–29)

In the gospel we have just heard, Jesus announces a "double" resurrection. The *dead* about whom he first speaks are men and women, which includes ourselves, who are alive on this earth but are destined to die. But among the living, who are destined for death, some are already *spiritually* dead, because they are sinners.

Sin is the real cause of death, because death, as St. Paul tells us, is "the wages of sin" (Rom 6:3). But so long as we journey on this earth, nothing is lost. God continues to offer us his forgiveness.

To those who are dead through sin, God offers to raise them, before they experience physical death. Jesus said: *I solemnly assure you the man who hears my word and has faith in him who sent me possesses eternal life.*

How is that possible? Because *eternal life* is God's very life. And God gave that life to his Son, who is also God. The Son, who is both God and man, can therefore communicate that life to humankind. For that to happen, men and women must be united to the Son by faith, by *hearing* his word.

Through faith, we entrust ourselves totally to God as our Father. And the life he shares with us here on earth is *eternal life.*

An hour is coming, has indeed come. Throughout our earthly life, a person can be converted and turn toward God by faith, impregnated with love for God and for our brothers and sisters. St. John says in another passage: "No need to be surprised . . . we have *passed from death to life* . . . because we love the brothers" (1 Jn 3:13–14, reading 29).

In the course of our lives, many of us have undergone periods of error and disorder—even times when we have forgotten God. If, perhaps close to our last hour, we hear

Christ's word, we can escape our state of death and *not come under condemnation*. On the last day, Christ's word will judge us, if we have rejected it. But if we have heard God's word, we escape the judgment, because we have listened to him who has come not to judge but to save (Jn 12:47–48).

This statement of Jesus' is so wonderful that he must say to his listeners: *No need for you to be surprised*. He immediately announced another wonder that is even more surprising: the miracle of the final, physical resurrection of people who have died in the strict sense, *those in their tombs*. At this point, Jesus again affirmed: *an hour is coming*—but he no longer adds, as previously, *has indeed come*.

This "total resurrection" will come at the end of time. But it begins now, and is present in the person of Jesus. At the sound of *his voice*, in obedience to his signal, *they will come forth* from *their tombs*. *Those who have done right* and obeyed his word *shall rise to live*.

This has already happened to them, but in the obscurity of faith. They will "enter life" in the sense that they will enjoy it with their whole being—in full light, and in a freedom which will no longer be restricted by the captivity of death and the grave.

St. John's first letter recalls the two stages of our resurrection. First, the obscure earthly stage: "Dearly beloved, we are God's children now; what we shall later be has not yet come to light." Then comes the luminous, heavenly stage: "We shall know it, when God's Son will appear we shall be like him, for we shall see him as he is" (1 Jn 3:2).

Our encounter with death quite naturally inspires sadness and mourning. We are plunged into night, into the unknown. But we have just heard Jesus' voice pierce the silence. We see his light through obscurity.

Let us be strengthened by the certitude that we have a Savior, who loves us and who has come for one purpose: to save us.

115. "I Will Raise Up Everyone on the Last Day"

(Jn 6: 37–40)

We have "lost" one of our own — a sad loss for us. And perhaps, while our brother was sick, there came a day when we had to acknowledge with fear in our hearts: "He is lost."

I call to mind the place of these words — *lose, loss* — in the vocabulary of death to help you notice that Jesus often used them in the Gospel, but always to reject them.

He described himself in relationship to the publican Zacchaeus, a sinner who was converted: "The Son of Man has come to search out and save what was lost" (Lk 19:10). On the night before he died, Jesus said to his Father: "I have not lost one of those you gave me" (Jn 18:9, see 17:12). He concluded the parable of the lost sheep in the same way: "It is no part of your heavenly Father's plan that a single one of these shall ever come to grief" (Mt 18:14).

Likewise in St. John, Jesus has just told us: *It is not to do my own will that I have come down from heaven, but to do the will of him who sent me. It is the will of him who sent me that I should lose nothing of what he has given me.*

Therefore the Father's will, like the Son's, is a loving will that must support our hope. The Father and Jesus do not will even one of Jesus' disciples to be lost.

But that doesn't say enough. Jesus is not satisfied with that negation. We are too inclined to view our own "salvation" in a negative way. In the Christian vocabulary, "being saved" is much more than escape from unhappiness and destruction. Therefore Jesus went on to say in our gospel: *It is the will of him who sent me that I should lose nothing of what he has given me; rather, that I should raise it up on the last day.* Indeed, for the person *who believes* in Jesus, salvation is perfect happiness, complete peace, *eternal life*, which means not only everlasting life but also the fullness of God's life.

But this fullness is given to us only if we are "raised up." We are not angels or pure spirits. We have a body. God has created our soul in a body. To be more precise, we *are* a body—no doubt an animated body, but a body. Death is characterized by loss of the body, because, separated from my soul, it's no longer my body—nor even a body at all. The body becomes "uniformed" matter, which decomposes.

My soul, on the other hand, was not created to live alone, as do the pure spirits. Through the body, the soul has acquired its thoughts, even the most noble and religious thoughts. With the body, the soul has worked, loved, sinned, and suffered.

Therefore, in order for the soul to be fully happy and fully itself, it must be reunited to its servant and work partner. For that reason, and in fulfillment of his Father's will, Jesus *will raise up all on the last day*. *All*, because there is no question of reward or selection, but of the need of human nature, which pertains to all humankind.

This is one of the most misunderstood doctrines, but also the most fundamental and most joyous doctrine of Christianity.

Again, I add an argument in favor of resurrection. Far from isolating and closing off our soul, as we often imagine, our body is a means of relationship and a communication instrument for the soul.

Through the body, we share in Jesus' humanity in the sacraments. But Jesus is risen. As God, he lives in heaven with his humanity, his glorified body. And so it is fitting that we remain in relationship with him in eternal life. How could that relationship and union be perfect, if we were forever deprived of our body!

On earth, it is through the body that we communicate with other people. We don't see or hear souls. We are united to souls by word and gesture, by services rendered, by radiant looks and smiles.

Before the resurrection, which will take place *on the last day*, we will not be anonymous phantoms, all alike and indistinguishable. Our charity and our love will have obtained heaven for us. Our measure of supernatural happiness will correspond to the degree of charity in which death finds us. Consequently, even "nude souls," if we can use such an expression, will be recognized by their spiritual physiognomy, molded by charity.

Above all, for those who are loved on earth—for "love never fails" (1 Cor 13:8)—the bonds of love, which will subsist in eternity, permit souls to be recognized and reunited. Bodily resurrection will also bring a fuller restitution of our personality.

Heaven is not a collection of happy individuals; it is a kingdom, a city, the New Jerusalem. Its social aspect, which will contribute to our happiness in heaven, requires that we possess a renewed and glorified body, which remains essential to the human nature that God has created.

We do not pretend to know in advance or with detail the manner in which so great a mystery will be realized. We merely seek a little understanding in order to increase our belief in the promise of Jesus, who has just reminded us: *I will raise them up on the last day.*

116. "Whoever Eats This Bread Will Live Forever"

(Jn 6:51–58)

We have come together to pray for our brother, who has just left us. The Mass will be celebrated for him, and many of you will share in the sacrifice of intercession through eucharistic communion. That seems to be obvious for Catholics. Nevertheless, we should not belittle these actions and see merely a religious gesture, which we can liken to lighting a vigil light, giving an alms, or making what we call a "little sacrifice."

On the contrary, the magnificent section of John's gospel, which we have just heard, teaches us that the mystery of the Mass, the Eucharist, is essentially related to the mystery of human death and resurrection, beginning with our Savior Jesus' death and resurrection.

Jesus begins with these words: *I am the living bread come down from heaven.* He also says, in the same discourse: "I myself am the bread of life" (6:35), and "God's bread comes down from heaven and gives life to the world" (6:33).

All these expressions have the same meaning. Jesus can be compared to bread, which is basic nourishment. He wants us to be united to him through faith and through eucharistic communion, which is "the mystery of faith."

Certainly, people eat to live; but Jesus is not referring to physical, earthly life. Because the bread descends from heaven, it is alive with the very life of God.

Just as the Father who has life sent me and I have life because of the Father, so the man who feeds on me will have life because of me. Therefore *if anyone eats this bread he shall live forever*—because the bread is Jesus, and Jesus shares with us the life of his Father who is "in heaven."

We should not believe that transmission of the Father's divine life to the Son and, consequently, the transmission of the Son's life to us through the eucharistic sacrament is a kind of physical, necessary flow, like the sun's radiating light or like sap that passes through a tree's roots and trunk to its branches. Between God and us was the disruption of sin, and it was necessary that Jesus reestablish communica-

tion between God and the human race. This is precisely
what Jesus did by his sacrifice.

When Jesus offered himself to the Father on our behalf,
he broke the bàrriers of sin and death. He reopened the
gates of life for us. This is what Jesus himself affirms when he
tells us: *The bread I will give is my flesh, for the life of the world.*

We must reconstruct that sentence to gain a better understanding: *The bread I will give is my flesh*, offered in sacrifice
in order to procure *the life of the world.*

We can ask how Jesus could conquer death by sub-
mitting to death, and how he could give us life by losing his
life on the cross. The reason lies in his sacrifice, which does
not end in death and burial. He had to achieve the *completion* of the sacrifice. He had to show, by resurrection, that his
sacrifice was a victory.

At Mass, we are not content merely in commemorating
and offering Jesus Christ's passion and death. Christ, whom
we make present by his own words under the appearance of
consecrated bread, is not a cadaver. He is the risen, living,
glorified Christ.

That is why our euchasristic communion unites us not
only to Jesus' death. Communion plants the seed of resurrection in us. Jesus tells us this in a formal way: *He who feeds
on my flesh and drinks my blood has life eternal, and I will raise him
up on the last day.*

Thus, by participating at this Mass—even better, by
going to Communion—we are united to the dead and risen
Jesus. In the obscure certainty of faith, we discover once
again our deceased brother, who has died in Jesus and who
must rise in him. Knowing that he led a Christian life and
that he faithfully shared in Christ's sacrifice, we trust that he
will be raised, and that we are raised ourselves, by virtue of
the Bread of Life. We will find our brother again in real
life, in eternal life.

117. "There Will Be One Flock, One Shepherd"

(Jn 10:14–16)

A principal disgrace and burden that death inflicts on us is dissolution and separation. Death separates us from those we love. Death separates our departed ones from us by removing them from our world. Is it not true that one of the greatest sadnesses of advanced age is that, little by little, we lose our contemporaries, our childhood companions, our school friends? Gradually, we sense we are alone: survivors of a declining generation.

Generally in the Gospel and particularly in the passage we have just heard, Jesus is represented as the Good Shepherd, who gathers his sheep. In St. Luke (15:3–7), Jesus is the shepherd who seeks out and leads back a stray sheep, because, apart from the flock and its leader, the stray would die of hunger or be devoured by savage beasts. Shortly after our reading, St. John says that Jesus had "to die . . . to gather into one all the dispersed children of God" (Jn 11:51, 52).

In fact, Jesus says in our reading: *For these sheep I will give my life.* He gives his life for them, and at the same time he shares his life with them. "I came that they may have life and have it to the full" (Jn 10:10). His sacrifice is not only an expiatory sacrifice, it is also a living and life-giving sacrifice.

Jesus nourishes his disciples by giving them his flesh to eat in the Eucharist (see Jn 6:53, reading 116). Just as the beginning of that divine life consists in faith (see Jn 6:29), Jesus speaks to them in order to nourish them with his word: His sheep "hear his voice" (Jn 10:3), because *he knows his sheep and his sheep know him.* Between Jesus and them is reciprocity, communion in knowledge and love, because

throughout the Bible "knowing" implies intimacy and loving dialogue.

Therefore we are strengthened when we face the sadness of death. In the obscurity of death, we are led by him
who is described in a psalm: "The Lord is my shepherd . . .
even though I walk in the dark valley I fear no evil; for you
are at my side with your rod and your staff that give me
courage" (Ps 22/23).

Therefore Jesus' true disciples, those who are part of his
sheepfold, are those who are guided by his word, which they
hear throughout their earthly life. They are nourished and
fortified by the eucharistic food he so generously gives them.
But what about the others? What about those who seem to
us to have lived at a distance from the Church and its teachings and practices? We would worry about their destiny if
we did not recall the second part of our gospel.

After Jesus spoke to the sheep who are obviously his own,
he added: *I have other sheep that do not belong to this fold. I must
lead them too.*

When Jesus spoke in that manner, he was surely thinking of the flock of Israel, which waited for the Messiah.
Didn't he say that he had been sent "after the lost sheep of the
house of Israel"?

The *other sheep* are evidently pagans. They too must be
saved, because "God wants all men to be saved and come to
know the truth" (1 Tm 2:4). And they must be saved by
Christ, because "there is no salvation in anyone else" (Acts
4:12).

After Jesus' ascension, the apostles were so obligated to
bring the Gospel to pagans that no longer was there a difference between Jews and pagans (see Gal 3:28, Col 3:11):
All would form *one flock*, because Jesus had to bring "salvation to the ends of the earth" (Acts 13:47).

Because God wants all men and women to be saved, we

should realize that Christ's salvation must reach the people who lived before him and the people who have never heard the Gospel proclaimed. In the prologue of the Fourth Gospel, St. John tells us that *the Word*, who is God's Son and the Light and Truth of the world, was "the real light which gives light to every man" (Jn 1:9).[16] Therefore we can think that the people who have lived outside the Church, the *other sheep that do not belong to this fold*, really (and perhaps without knowing it) have *heard the voice* of the Good Shepherd by obeying their conscience, by seeking the Truth, and by placing themselves at the service of their brothers and sisters.

We are not separated even from these "outsiders." On the contrary, death has destroyed the visible barriers that brought division into our lives. Now nothing stands in the way of our being reunited in *one flock*, guided by *one shepherd*.

118. "I Am the Resurrection"

(Jn 11:17–27)

The gospel we have just heard is quite appropriate for the occasion that brings us together. We are reminded of a dialogue between Jesus and Martha. This Bethany family— two sisters, Mary and Martha, and their brother, Lazarus— had a house in which Jesus often received hospitality. There he was able to relax, in the peace of simple friendship, when he faced attacks and misunderstandings.

Lazarus has just died, in Jesus' absence. Martha, who *went to meet Jesus*, spoke to him in a way that proved her trust in him. She knew he had cured many sick people and that he cared for those in misery. *Lord, if you had been here, my brother would never had died.* Martha said this only in regret, not as a reproach.

However, can't we recognize in her the beginning of

that rebellion which threatens to overcome us when one of
our loved ones dies? Couldn't God, *shouldn't* God, have done
something to prevent this? It's as though God must be at our
beck and call, dispensing us from every trial in life and pre-
venting the death of those we love. All this despite the fact
that death—yes, premature death as well—is the lot of all
men and women.

Despite Martha's sorrow, despite her ignorance about
Jesus' absence, she maintained a very firm hope, though she
had not determined exactly what that hope is: *Even now I am
sure that God will give you whatever you ask of him.*

Jesus' response was categorical, but he made no promise
for the immediate future: *Your brother will rise again.*

Then Martha expressed the conviction of all religious
Jews: "*I know he will rise again in the resurrection on the last day,*
when all men and women will be raised up." This is a real
profession of faith. Note the formula: *I know.*

And yet that is not enough for Jesus. Martha's faith was
too distant and general. Martha must know that the resurrection will be the work of Jesus, her friend, who is speaking
to her at this moment. However, it does not suffice to believe
in an abstraction, in a general idea, but *in the resurrection.* Her
belief must be in a concrete, living person—Jesus.

He is the one who gives resurrection. He had said it on
several occasions: "Whoever believes in me I will raise up
on the last day" (see Jn 6:39, 40, 44, 45). But now Jesus used
a much more surprising expression, which is found nowhere
else in the New Testament: "*I am the resurrection and the life.*"

Jesus is not only the Person who bestows resurrection
and life; he *is*, in person, resurrection and life.

In fact, we can use the word *resurrection* for the many
people who were raised up earlier by prophets and, more
recently, by Jesus. For instance, Jesus is about to raise up
his friend, Lazarus. But the earlier resurrections by prophets
were nothing more than announcements, and very imperfect

images, of real resurrection, because the raised people will die again, this time for good. But "once raised from the dead, Christ will never die again" (Rom 6:9).

Jesus' resurrection is the unique resurrection, from which all other resurrections flow. He is the Risen One *par excellence*. All who will be raised will come to life in and through him. This is what Jesus wants us to understand when he makes the strange statement: *I am the resurrection and the life.*

Jesus goes on to say: *Whoever believes in me, though he should die, will come to life; and whoever is alive and believes in me will never die.* Belief in the risen Jesus means to belong to him and thus to share in his resurrection.

Let us respond to Jesus, as did Martha, who mourned her beloved brother's death: *Yes, Lord, I have come to believe that you are the Son of God: he who is to come into the world.* Then we will have a faith that is alive, concrete, immediate. We will have a faith that will help us overcome all the anguish that death imparts in us.

119. Jesus Raises His Friend, Lazarus

(Jn 11:32b–45 [Long Form]
Jn 11:32b–36, 41–45 [Short Form])

Christians are faithful to the baptismal credo, as well as to the Creed they recite every Sunday at Mass, because they believe "in the resurrection of the body" (Apostles' Creed) and they await "the resurrection of the dead and the life of the world to come" (Creed of Nicea-Constantinople). That is their belief.

For Christians, resurrection is not a "far out" possibility or an optimistic hypothesis. Resurrection is a certainty that strengthens them in the presence of death.

Does this mean that death is an unimportant passage, about which we can have no fear or sorrow?

I am quite aware that some believers are of the opinion that Christian funerals must be joyfully celebrated with festival adornments: flowers and the sung Alleluia. Such celebration, however, would be cruel for the mourning relatives and not in conformity with true belief. Our deceased are sinners. We must pray for them before we rejoice for their death. Even if they are saints, we should not confuse their "funeral" with "canonization."

Faith, which helps us share in God's certitudes, must not render us inhuman; and Jesus gave us an example in this regard. We have seen him in the account of Lazarus' resurrection. Jesus *knew* he would raise Lazarus, how can *we* be certain of that?

Before giving the order, *Lazarus, come out!*, Jesus said, *looking upward:* "*Father, I thank you for having heard me. I know that you always hear me.*" Despite Jesus' certitude in the miracle, he approached the tomb and *was moved by the deepest emotions.*

The Evangelist also reports that Jesus was *troubled in spirit* when he *approached the tomb.*[17] When the tomb was pointed out to him, *Jesus began to weep, which caused the Jews to remark, "See how much he loved him!"*

Jesus is indeed God. He knew that his Father *always hears him*, and therefore he knew that he himself would raise up Lazarus (see Heb 5:7).

But at the same time, Jesus is truly human: he shared every human weakness. He knew fatique (Jn 4:6), hunger (Mt 4:2 and parallel texts, 21:18, and Lk 11:12), amazement (Mt 8:10), surprise (Mk 6:6), anger (Mk 3:5), trouble (Jn 11:33, 12:37, 13:21), sadness, anguish, and fear as he confronted his death (Mt 26:37 and parallel texts).

Finally, he wept. Only two times do the evangelists report Jesus' tears.[18] When he gazed at Jerusalem and announced its destruction, he wept because Jerusalem was his fatherland (see Lk 19:41). He also wept before the tomb of his friend, Lazarus. Jesus loved Lazarus and his sister, Martha (Jn 11:5), and was deeply moved when he saw Mary, Lazarus' other sister, in tears (Jn 11:33).

Shall we be less human than our Master? Firm as our faith may be, how can we believe that its divine science forbids us to weep? Surely, as St. Paul says, "If our hopes in Christ are limited to this life only, we are the most pitiable of men. But as it is, Christ is now raised from the dead, the first fruits of those who have fallen asleep" (1 Cor 15:19–20).

Therefore faith and hope must lessen our sadness. But faith and hope should not suppress sadness, because they do not destory charity. We have seen that Jesus shared the sadness of his friends, Mary and Martha, and wept for Lazarus, because he loved all three of them. And St. Paul recommended fraternal charity and hospitality to the Romans when he told them to "rejoice with those who rejoice, weep with those who weep" (Rom 12:15).

As Christians, therefore, let us be believing and hope-filled men and women, who believe in the resurrection of the dead and await that resurrection with confidence. As we wait, let us not be embarrassed when we weep for the loss of our friends, and when we weep with our friends!

120. The Grain that Dies Bears Fruit

(Jn 12:24–28 [Long Form]
Jn 12:24–26 [Short Form])

Jesus' words, which we have just heard, contain a precious teaching on his death and the death of Christians. He said these words only a few days before he died on the cross, on Palm Sunday. He had just made a triumphal entry into Jerusalem,—with the acclaim of the crowds.

Greeks who were sympathetic to the Jewish religion had made a pilgrimage to the holy city to ask to meet this prestigious man, and Jesus knew that his Church would soon extend throughout the Greek world, which was synonymous with the civilized world. But the "glory" in question would be obtained only at the price of his death. He illustrated this law of spiritual productivity through a short parable: *I solemnly assure you, unless the grain of wheat falls to the earth and dies, it remains just a grain of wheat. But if it dies, it produces much fruit.*

Jesus, of course, does not mean that death itself is the cause of life. If *the grain of wheat* which *falls to the earth* really died, it would bear no fruit and would be completely lost, and thus we represent death as an end, an annihilation, a total loss. Rather, Jesus' parable suggests that, according to God's will and plan, death is the condition of life, because death is the door to resurrection.

Death, which seems to us to be a difficult constraint and an enslavement (see Rom 6:16–23), is in reality a liberation. Similarly, the grain of wheat, which *seems* to die in the earth, will break through the shell that surrounds it, in order to burst forth into a multitude of other living wheat grains on living stalks.

To respond to the question of unbelievers, "How are the dead to be raised up? What kind of body will they have?" (1 Cor 15:35), St. Paul used the same comparison that Jesus did: "The seed you sow does not germinate unless it dies" (1 Cor 15:36). The law of death—the road toward resurrection and true life—is applicable first of all to Jesus himself: his death will save the entire human race.

The same law is applicable for us and for our dead. They disappeared, before our very eyes, and were buried in the ground like a grain of wheat. But their death can be the entry into a life that is infinitely more intense and productive.

How many families experience the death of their father or mother as a hopeless disaster! Little by little, the family discovers that the one who has disappeared has become advisor, protector, and intercessor in a much greater way than he or she was during this earthly life. St. Therese of the Child Jesus announced that she would spend her heaven doing good deeds on earth. And she kept her word!

Can we believe that every death is fruitful?

We must be careful to see the parable of the grain, fallen into the ground, as a comparison, not as a demonstration. The grain that decomposes in the earth *produces much fruit* by virtue of a natural, necessary process. The world's salvation was enacted through Jesus' death because his death was offered freely, through love, which made it a meritorious sacrifice, and the same is true of the death of Christians. That is why Jesus told the parable of the grain of wheat and completed it with an application for ourselves: *The man who loves his life loses it.*

Loving one's life—living in selfishness, refusing to serve God and one's brothers and sisters—means to *lose one' life.* How could death be positive and productive if it merely brings an end to a life of selfishness?

On the other hand, *the man who hates his life in this world preserves it to life eternal*, because a life of such detachment and service is free, loving, and complete: *life eternal* has already begun.

Eternal life! How can we imagine what it is? How can we desire it?

Jesus gives us the simplest definition of eternal life: *If anyone would serve me, let him follow me*, let him be my disciple and imitator. *Where I am, there will my servant be.*

Eternal life—heaven—is "being with Jesus," as Jesus promised the "good thief," his companion in the crucifixion on Calvary: "I assure you: this day you will be with me in paradise" (Lk 23:43, reading 111; the same idea is in Jn 14:3, reading 121, and Jn 17:24, reading 122).

This section of the gospel has been used for the Masses of martyrs: a martyr being one who truly follows Jesus, even to the voluntary sacrifice of one's own life.[19] Can we apply this very demanding text of Jesus to someone who, like us, is one of the vast number of average Christians? Yes, we can, because many lives that appear to be ordinary or mediocre are lived in modest, everyday heroism, which supposes much love.

Another reason is that, at the moment of death, Jesus may open the eyes of the persons he calls and strengthen them so that (with the help of grace) death becomes a supreme act of detachment from this world.

Is it possible that a Christian, who has assisted at Mass with even minimal attention, does not understand that the Mass is a realization of the mystery of one's personal sacrifice, offered in union with Christ's sacrifice?

Today, therefore, let us pray that the person we are about to bury in *the earth*, like *the grain of wheat*, may see the offering of his life accepted by Jesus. Having followed Jesus throughout his life, even in difficult times, may our deceased brother be with Jesus in eternal life.

In the last part of our gospel, Jesus is described as deeply *troubled* by the thought of his approaching death. Because he was fully human, the thought of death made him tremble and back away. He was tempted, for a moment, to ask his Father to spare him the trial—the "cup," as he will say a few days later at Gethsemane (Mk 14:36, reading 106). But he reconsidered and accepted his Father's will by affirming, once again, the fruitfulness of his death.

For Jesus, death was be a homage rendered to God, and because of that very fact his death saved humanity.

Father, glorify your name. And the Father responded: *I*

have glorified it—especially by all the miracles Jesus has accomplished and by all the truth that he revealed throughout his short life.

And I will glorify it again—by Jesus' resurrection, by the expansion of the Church under the impulse of the Holy Spirit.

Yes, death is promise, death is hope. The grain, buried in the ground, *if it dies produces much fruit.*

121. "I Am the Way, the Truth, and the Life"

(*Jn 14:1–6*)

The gospel we have just heard is taken from the farewell discourse that Jesus addressed to his disciples a few hours before his death. He had already made the announcement of Judas' betrayal (Jn 13:21–30), his own departure (13:31–33), and Peter's denial (13:36–38). These announcements troubled their hearts, just as we are troubled by the imminent death of someone we love. That is why he told them: *Do not let your hearts be troubled.*

Therefore let us listen to the comforting words spoken by Jesus, so that we can profit from them.

Have faith in God and faith in me. Belief in God is good and necessary, but is not sufficient. God can seem so distant! We must also believe in Jesus, who is God Omnipotent. But he is also our brother, who is very near and compassionate.

In my Father's house there are many dwelling places; otherwise, how could I have told you that I was going to prepare a place for you?

We often take the phrase, "in the Father's house," to mean that there are many rooms. This seems to mean that there are several ways of being truly Christian, or even that there are different degrees of heavenly happiness; but this is not what the text means. Jesus' words mean simply that the

Father's house is open to everyone, because "he wants all men to be saved" (1 Tm 2:4).

Jesus continues: *I am indeed going to prepare a place for you, and then I shall come back to take you with me, that where I am you also may be.* Let us not therefore, represent death as an agonizing plunge into an unknown abyss. Jesus comes to seek us out so that we might be with him forever.

This is indeed a comfort; but Jesus says even more: *You know the way that leads where I go.* To which St. Thomas, the disciple who wants precise answers and certainty (see Jn 20:24–29), replies with the question: *Lord, we do not know where you are going. How can we known the way?*

Jesus' response is well known, but today his words should be especially striking and should quiet all our restlessness: *I am the way, the truth, and the life; no one comes to the Father but through me.*

Jesus is the only Savior (see Acts 4:12). The *Way*, by which our absent friend has departed, is Jesus. The *Truth*, whom our friend has just encountered as he left the shadows and doubts of our human condition, is Jesus. And the *Life*, into which our friend has entered, having passed through death, is Jesus.

Whatever weaknesses he had in life, our friend was a believer. He has fulfilled his baptismal commitments. He has fallen asleep in Christ (see 1 Cor 15:18); he has died with the Lord (see Rom 6:8) and for the Lord (see Rom 14:8). He has followed *the Way*; he has discovered *the Truth*; he has entered *the Life*!

122. "I Want Them to Be with Me"

(*Jn 17: 1–3, 24–26* [*Long Form*]
Jn 17: 1a, 24–26 [*Short Form*])

Christians are convinced that we should pray for those who are in their "last agony," so that they may be victorious in overcoming the most awesome trial: death. Christians also believe that we must pray for the dead, so that, as soon as possible, they may reach the kingdon of pure light and perfect joy.

We have come together today for the purpose of praying for the one who has just left us. But of what value are our prayers when someone stands before the mystery of "the beyond," which is so obscure?

Let us not allow ourselves to be disturbed by such unrest. The gospel passage that we have just heard is from the supreme prayer that Jesus addressed to his Father only a few hours before his death.

In the beginning of the prayer, Jesus implores the Father: *Father, the hour has come* — who had said to his mother at Cana: "My hour has not yet come" (Jn 2:4). Now, he has revealed the Father by his teachings, his miracles, his entire person. *The hour has come* to accomplish the supreme sacrifice, which consists not only in his death on the cross but also in his resurrection. That is why he asks the Father: *Give glory to your Son*. His prayer was not prompted by vanity or self-interest, because he continues: *that your Son may give glory to you.*

Jesus was speaking not only of the reciprocal relationship between Father and Son but also of the salvation which Christ's sacrifice brings to his human sisters and brothers, at the same time that he glorified his Father: "So *that the Son may bestow eternal life on those you gave him.*"

We should not try to represent eternal life with fairy-tale imagery. In this text, indeed, we have a definition that is both simple and magnificent: *Eternal life is this: to know you, the only true God, and him whom you have sent, Jesus Christ.*

Knowing does not have merely a theoretical or scholarly meaning here. Jesus refers to knowledge that is animated by love, that reaches fulfillment in communion. Thus St. John, the apostle, writes elsewhere: "The man without love has known nothing of God, for God is love" (1 Jn 4:8).

No doubt God is mysterious and difficult to know: "No one has ever seen God. It is God the only Son, ever at the Father's side, who has revealed him" (Jn 1:18).

When we know Jesus whom the Father *has sent*, we therefore *know the only true God*. This, already is *eternal life*, possessed (like an embryo) in a very obscure but very real manner.

What very great hope we must have whenever we see a Christian die. The deceased was sinful and imperfect, but we cannot doubt his sincerity!

The conclusion of the prayers concerns us directly. At the moment Jesus died, he prayed for us by thinking of our death. And with what authority he prayed! *Father, all those you gave me*—all those whom the Father attracted (see Jn 6:44) by giving them the grace to become Jesus' disciples— *all those you gave me I would have in my company where I am, to see this glory of mine.*

Have you noticed that Jesus said *I would?* Nowhere else in the Gospel, and particularly when Jesus addresses his Father, does he speak with such authority: *I would.* And what is it that he wants? That we be *in his company.*

Jesus is going to die. Through his love-filled death he merits entry into glory; but he does not wish to be the only human to make such entry. He wishes that all of his own be *in his company.*

For us, it is clear that happiness is being *in Jesus' company*. Moreover, it is no exaggeration to add that Jesus' happiness would be incomplete if those whom the Father gave him to save were not with Jesus, who came to save all men and women (see Jn 3:16–17, reading 113). The Father's glory does not derive from Jesus' pride in his triumph, which is to enter heaven as the Leader of all the believers whom he has redeemed (see Eph 1:21–23, 4:9–13).

Jesus completes the prayer by describing the purpose of his incarnation, his life on earth and his death: *that your love for me may live in them, and I may live in them.* A perfect and reciprocal knowledge; an intimate and lasting love; a joyous, complete, and indissoluble union—this is the meaning of the *eternal life* that Jesus asks of his Father on our behalf at the very moment he begins his walk toward Calvary.

How can we doubt for one moment that such a prayer, said for us, would be heard? And how can we not unite ourselves to that prayer with absolute confidence?

123. At the Foot of Jesus' Cross

(Jn 19:17ab, 18, 25–30)

If the death of one of our brothers and sisters causes us sadness and agony, if we are downcast by the prospect of our own, inevitable death, nothing can bring greater peace to our hearts than the description of the way in which Jesus Christ, our Model and Guide, approached death. That is why on their deathbeds, many saints wanted to hear a Gospel account of our Savior's death. That is why a crucifix is placed on caskets and graves. That is why we have just heard the reading of a section of "St. John's Passion."

Jesus carried the cross by himself. We know that the other evangelists describe how Simon of Cyrene helped Jesus carry the cross—but Roman law demanded that the condemned person carry his own cross. Surely Jesus, who voluntarily accepted death, carried his cross part of the way. But as Jesus said earlier: "Whoever wishes to be my follower must deny his very self, take up his cross each day, and follow in my footsteps" (Lk 9:23).

If our cross seems heavy today, let us think of Jesus, who carried his cross in order to give us an example.

Jesus was not alone on the cross. On each side were men who were crucified with him. One of them received Jesus' promise of being with him in paradise that very day. Also some faithful followers stood *near the cross*. Everyone, therefore, had not abandoned him. Several sympathetic women were there, and *his mother with the disciple whom Jesus loved*. In the agony of death, it is a great comfort to be surrounded by those we love.

Mary was there, silent and loving, and we who suffer should recall what she suffered. We should realize that she understands us, not only because of her experience of sorrow or her motherly compassion; she understands us because Jesus, at his supreme hour, *confided* us to her in the person of the disciple Jesus loved. This disciple personified every disciple who would come to Jesus, till the end of the world.

In fact, Jesus was not primarily concerned with finding support for the mother he would leave behind. Indeed, Jesus made Mary the "mother" of all his disciples, all who will put his word into practice and continue his work: *Woman, there is your son.* Only then did he say to the disciple: *"There is your mother." From that hour onward, the disciple took her into his care.*

These words are very simple but very moving, especially because *the disciple* in question is the writer, John the

Evangelist, "whom Jesus loved, the one who had leaned against Jesus' chest during the supper" on Holy Thursday (Jn 21:20).

Since that time, Christ's entire Church considers Mary our Mother, recalls her sufferings on Calvary and her great courage, and petitions her as "Consoler of the Afflicted" (Litany of Loretto).

Now that Jesus has given his farewell to those who loved him most and to those who were closest to him, he complained of thirst—a frequent complaint of those who die, especially those who suffer copious bleeding through flagellation and crucifixion: *I am thirsty*. Jesus drank the vinegar that the soldiers offered him. Then he died, saying: *Now it is finished*—like a good worker at the end of a day, like a priest who has celebrated his sacrifice.

In fact, St. John had reported Jesus' words earlier: "No one takes my life from me; I lay it down freely" (Jn 10:18). This is why the Evangelist used a very special expression to describe Jesus' death: *He delivered over his spirit*.

St. John's account of Jesus' death manifests great serenity and peace. However, it is not easy for us to react in the same way to the death of those we love intimately. We are always tempted, if not to rebel against God, to regard him as cruel and unjust. Even though the deaths of simple people cannot be as voluntary as Jesus', let us, the survivors, try to make an offering of those deaths.

In the beginning, "God did not make death" (Wis 1:13); but because man sinned, death was introduced in God's plans. (It was, of course, foreseen by God's providence.) Of itself, death is no more than loss and destruction; through love, it can become a sacrifice that obtains blessing and peace, which is the profound meaning of the Mass we are offering. The Mass makes Christ's death present, with his intention of making an offering, a sacrifice, of infinite value.

Let us join our very human and very justified sorrow to
Christ's sacrifice so that our sacrifice becomes his. Then we
will be able to say, as he did, in the presence of the Virgin
Mary: *Now it is finished.*

For us, this means "I have arrived at a loving acceptance of God's will. I have made this suffering and this loss a
source of peace and a contribution to the salvation and happiness of all my brothers and sisters."

1. In fact, we generally count just eight beatitudes. The "ninth
blessed" (in verse 11) seems to constitute a repeat of the Eighth Beatitude,
but with a new structure. This "beatitude," by itself, does not announce
its reward. Another reason for counting the two as a single beatitude is
that the structure goes from third person to second person: "Happy will
you be . . . ," which is a transition between the beatitudes in the strict sense
and the remainder of the Sermon on the Mount, which continues through
its conclusion (7:21) in the second person.

2. Nevertheless, the lectionary (and Osty) translates in verse 11:
Happy will you be. But the Greek verb (Jesus surely used the Aramean verb)
is in the present: *Happy are you.* The Jerusalem Bible (like the TOB)
retained the present tense. But surprisingly, in the TOB French text, the
present tense is followed by a future: "Happy are you when you will be
insulted . . ." The subordinate verb and the two verbs that follow are
indeed in the future in the Greek text, but they are preceded by the
conjunction ὥταν, which implies eventuality. The correct translation
appears in the lectionary: "*if* they persecute you . . ."

3. The lectionary (and the Jerusalem Bible) translates: *Your reward
will be great in heaven.* Osty and the TOB have the present tense: "is great."
We cannot be certain about the tense, because the Greek text has no verb.
We favor the present tense, because the reward should not be given only
at a later time. The reward is already prepared and reserved, according
to an ideal frequently expressed in the New Testament (see Mt. 25:34,
Lk 12:33, 2 Tm 4:8, 1 Pt 1:4).

4. That is how Luke 17:21 can be translated in a way that is too
interiorized: "The kingdom of God is within you." The lectionary, the
TOB, the Jerusalem Bible, and Osty: "The kingdom of God is in your
midst."

5. We follow the lectionary translation, which is also that of the
TOB. The usual translation, "sheep and bucks," loses sight of the fact that
there are no flocks of bucks and that the difference in sexes means nothing

in this passage. The word εριφος (*haedus* in Latin) means precisely a lamb
(see Lk 15:29). Jeremiah explains that each night the shepherd separates
the sheep, who can pass the night outside, from the more fragile lambs.

6. We received inspiration primarily from J. Dupont's "L'Eglise et la
pauvreté," in *L'Eglise de Vatican II*, vol. II ("Unam Sanctam," 51b), pp.
339–372, and from J. Jeremias' "The Parables of Jesus," pp. 196–200. For
Dupont, "the little ones who are my brothers" are all who suffer, without
distinction. For Jeremias, this scene is a response to the problem of the
salvation of the pagans. See op. cit. and Jeremias' "Jésus et les paiens"
(*Cahiers Théologiques* 39), pp. 42, 57, 60–62. The same universal interpretation is held by X. Léjon-Dufour in *Les Evangiles et l'histoire de Jésus*, p.
425; by P. Bonnard and W. Trilling in their commentaries on Matthew;
and by Schnackenburg and Feuillet.

Others say that "brothers" refers to Christ's disciples, and more
precisely to the evangelizing missionaries. See S. Légasse, "Jésus et
l'enfant" (*Etudes Bibliques*), pp. 85–100. In "Assemblés du Seigneur"
(65, pp. 17–28), A. Duprez cites Cerfaux and Winandy and others who
hold the latter opinion.

The latter opinion, which seems to us to be less traditional than the
first, lends itself more easily to homily preparation.

7. The same series of events is found in the Synoptic Gospels:
Mk 10:17–31 = Mt 19:16–30 = Lk 18:18–30. And yet our reading
from Mark has some unique aspects that deserve our attention. Mark
adds "and for the sake of the gospel"; Mark also specifies "the hundredfold." He repeats the enumeration of the things the apostles have left, for
which Jesus promises the hundredfold reward: "homes, brothers, etc."
Mark also adds "with persecutions." Finally, with Luke, Mark dis-
tinguishes between "the time that is already here" and "the age of the
world to come."

8. See J. Jeremias, "Paroles de Jesus . . . le Notre Pere" (*Lectio
Divina*, 38), p. 68. Also *Foi Vivante*, 7.

9. See P. Benoit, "Passion et Resurrection du Seigneur" (*Lire la
Bible*, 6), p. 222.

10. Bossuet, *Oeuvres oratoires*, ed. critique Lebarq-Urbain-Levesque,
IV: 158–159. *Sermon sur la Purification de la Sainte Vièrge*, the first point,
Lent at Louvre, 1662.

11. Matthew prepares for the statement "the dead rise" by his earlier
account of the resurrection of Jairus' daughter. Luke has already given the
account of the raising of the son of the widow of Naim.

12. The liturgy of martyrs contains a translation error: "Precious in
the eyes of the Lord is the death of his holy ones." Rather than "precious,"
we should understand the meaning to be "costly" or "burdensome":
"Costly in the eyes of the Lord is the death of his holy ones."

13. In the "eschatological discourses": Mt 24:42, 43, 44, Mt 25:13, Mk 13:33, 34, 35, 37, Lk 17:26-29 (for the meaning of "watchfulness," without use of the word); Lk 21:34-36.

14. The Vulgate translates verse 35 as "have your lighted lamp *in hand*," an unfortunate addition; such a posture would make all work impossible. The literal Greek text says: "Let your loins be girt and your lamps lit." The situation of these servants is not that of Mt 25's ten young women, who had nothing to do but wait with their lamps in hand.

15. See Mt 26:38, 40, 41, Mk 14:34, 37, 38. Although Luke's narrative does not mention watchfulness, it twice contains the advice: "Pray so that you will not enter into temptation" (22:40 and 22:46). Luke does not stress the sleep of the disciples.

16. For the universal interpretation of the enlightenment the Word brings to "every man and woman," see A. Feuillet, *Le prologue du quatrieme evangile* (Paris, 1968), pp. 67ff; also, in a briefer treatment, M. E. Boismard, *Le prologue de saint Jean* (Paris, 1953) (*Lectio Divina*, 11), p. 48. These two authors adopt the translation also used in the lectionary: "who enlightens all men who come into the world."

17. Without complement, the verb the evangelist uses ($εμβριμαομαι$) means "to growl within oneself," and with the complement the verb means "to reprimand" someone (see Mt 9:30, Mk 14:5). The Greek fathers (Origen, Chrysostom, and others) understood this to mean that Jesus manifested his anger. But against whom? Against death? Against those who wept in despair? Against excessive mourning? The context suggests nothing of the sort. Rather, the context suggests the verb's translation as "to tremble with emotion," as in the Vulgate and in the majority of French translations (see Fr. Lagrange's *Commentary* on this verse). Although the French lectionary's translation is not literal, it makes sense.

18. Besides, the Letter to the Hebrews (5:7) tells us that Christ "offered prayers and supplications with loud cries and tears to God who was able to save him from death." From all appearances, the text alludes to Gethsemane.

19. In the preconciliar Roman Missal, verses 24-26 constituted the gospel for two great martyrs: St. Ignatius of Antioch, because he called himself "God's wheat" (Rom 4:1), and St. Lawrence, because he was a deacon. In verse 26, "serving" translates the Greek $διακονειν$. The Greek $διακονος$ is translated by "servant." The lectionary of the postconciliar missal retained these two attributions of the text, which were also used in the Common of Martyrs.

FOR FUNERALS OF CHILDREN

Here we give the commentary of three pericopes used exclusively for funerals of children. The complete list of readings, including those that are used either in their entirety or in part for adult funeral liturgies, can be found in the "Useful Notes" section (which begins on page 23).

The reader will note that the word "children" conforms to the Latin word *infantes*, which means "those who do not speak," or at least "those who have not reached the age of reason." For such *infantes*, the ritual for the baptism of "little children" (infants) had been used.

64. "Blessed Be God"

(Eph 1 : 3–5)

St. Paul has just invited us to "bless God," which means to praise and thank *the God and Father of our Lord Jesus Christ*. But God has taken away a little baby, who promised so much joy and embodied so much hope. How can we thank God, who has inflicted such a difficult trial on a family?

The Bible speaks highly of Job, a holy man of ancient times, who in a series of catastrophes lost not only his immense fortune but all of his children as well. When Job's wife advised him to curse God, Job replied: "The Lord gave and the Lord has taken away; blessed be the name of the Lord!" (Job 1:21).

St. Paul does not ask such heroism of us. Nevertheless, he invites us to bless God because Paul sees beyond the present misfortune. When Paul wrote this letter, he was not in a comfortable situation. He was undergoing a difficult imprisonment. And not only was he a prisoner, chained and exposed to death, his apostolate was curtailed.

Despite these setbacks, Paul says: *Blessed be God*, because he sees beyond his present trial. He considers and admires God's plan: *God has bestowed on us in Christ every spiritual blessing in the heavens*. When Paul says *in the heavens*, he does not mean that our earthly sadness is compensated by a joy that will come from heaven. Paul means that the *blessing* is *in Christ*: the blessing is connected with Jesus Christ, who, through his resurrection and ascension, is happy and victorious *in the heavens*. Paul goes on to explain: *God chose us in him before the world began, to be holy and blameless in his sight, to be full of love*.

That sentence surely concerns our baptism. Indeed, baptism makes it possible for us to live *in Christ Jesus*. Baptism makes us God's children, Christ's brothers and sisters, Christ's members.

Furthermore, baptism makes us other Christs. Therefore God calls us *to be holy and blameless in his sight*.

Unfortunately, when we look at ourselves, we are
aware that we have been unfaithful to that call. We are
neither *holy* nor *blameless*. But just the opposite can be said of
the small child whom God has taken to himself in the intact
holiness of infant baptism.

God has *predestined* all of *us to be his adopted sons and
daughters through Jesus Christ*. God follows a plan that we do
not understand. But if we have faith, we must believe that,
in whatever God does, whatever he allows to happen, God
acts according to his loving *will and pleasure*, because "God
did not make death" (Wis 1:13).

Surely God does not reproach us for our tears. But he
invites us, despite our sadness, to try to understand, in the
light of faith, that this small child, whom we mourn, is
called to heavenly glory and happiness. We are certain that
God's loving plan is infallibly realized in this regard. We also
believe that this little child, who has preceded us into
heaven, will guide and protect us and inspire us.

Thanks to this child, whom we will meet in heaven on
some future day, we are able to say, despite all that has
happened, with tears in our eyes: *Praised be the God and Father
of our Lord Jesus Christ*.

68. God Will Dry Every Tear

(*Rv 7:9–10, 15–17*)

St. John's Apocalypse, which we admit is a terrifying
book, filled with calamities and catastrophies, gives an
especially comforting portrayal of heaven in the mourning
that affects us today. Contrary to preachers in the past, who

affirmed "the small number of the elect," St. John shows heaven to be filled with *a huge crowd which no one could count:* a crowd of people who are victorious, because they *stand before the throne* of God, who created them, and *before the Lamb,* who redeemed them. They stand *in long white robes,* which, like white baptismal robes, are signs of victory, and *hold palm branches in their hands* to celebrate their triumph. Even our little ones, whose death inflicts us with intense mourning, are victorious and happy in the great heavenly assembly.

They do not form an amorphous, anonymous, gloomy crowd but, rather, a joyous crowd, filled with God's complete joy: *He who sits on the throne will give them shelter.* This means they will live in intimate personal relationships with God. *The Lamb,* Jesus Christ, who is on *the throne because he himself is God will lead them to the springs of life-giving water.* Small children who die, who seem to us so little, so unknowing, so unaware of everything, will be satisfied by drinking from *the springs of life-giving water.*

This means that they know God—they know him this moment—directly and without any intermediary. They will share—they already share—in the fullness of God's happiness, which is like *springs of water* that flow, refresh, and are *life giving.* For God is not a kind of puzzle. He is constantly renewed and inexhaustible happiness.

And God will wipe every tear from their eyes. Their death has made our tears flow more copiously than even their own, baby tears. And so we can translate that wonderful promise this way: *God will wipe every tear from our eyes.* When we rediscover these small children, when we see how happy and glorious these little ones are, we will share in their happiness and glory.

Today is a time for tears; but we must live in hope of the day when our tears will be wiped away by God's tenderness, which eludes us today. It may even appear that God is cruel. But on that day we will fully experience God and will recognize in reality, beyond all appearances to the contrary, that "God is love" (1 Jn 4:16).

124. The Greatest in the Kingdom of Heaven

(*Mt 18; 1–5, 10*)

On this very day, when we suffer the loss of a small child, Jesus has told us how great a tiny child is in his eyes and in God's eyes.

We might be tempted to consider a child an insignificant, an anonymous being, because he has not manifested any personality, nor has he rendered any service to society. Naturally, however, that's not the way his parents think. To them, this tiny child, who had attained only a bit of consciousness, brought great hope.

Why does Jesus declare so solemnly: *Unless you change and become like little children, you will not enter the kingdom of God?* Not because small children affect us by their innocence and their cute behavior. This sensitivity to children, so characteristic of our modern age, was completely foreign to people in ancient times. For them, a child was an inferior, negligible creature.

That is precisely the reason why children became a model for Jesus. In passages in earlier gospels, Jesus announced his passion. He taught that he had come to make himself small and to serve. But the disciples did not understand that lesson. On the contrary, they argued about who among them would be *of greatest importance in the kingdom of God*, which Jesus would establish.

Jesus, however, ordered his disciples to *change*, to renounce their ambitions and pretenses in order to *become like little children*. To Jesus, what is admirable and worthy of imitation is simplicity, refusal to be selfish, obedience and trust.

Consequently, *whoever makes himself lowly, becoming like this child, is of greatest importance in that heavenly reign.* Children, therefore, are *of greatest importance in the kingdom of God*, because in them is no pretense, no resistance to God's will. Therefore we must not *despise one of these little ones.*

No longer speaking only of children in the strict sense, Jesus speaks of those who resemble children. Those who are "small in age" may be despised by adult men and women, just as adults despise those who are "small" by their poverty, simplicity, and even their ignorance. But God does not despise them! On the contrary, *their angels in heaven constantly behold my heavenly Father's face.*

Therefore Jesus understands that parents suffer in losing a small creature, who has such value in the Father's eyes. Jesus came to give his life for children, just as he gave his life for illustrious adults, who often are the greatest sinners. Jesus, nonetheless, tells us to trust in his Father's goodness toward these little ones. The Father cares for them as he cares for all "children"—infinitely more than he cares for the birds of the air (see Mt 10:29–31)—because "children" are called to the eternal happiness of living intimately with the Father.

Because the Father invites us to imitate children, let us strive, in this ordeal, to trust in the Father, to believe in his goodness, and to throw ourselves into his arms like little children. And, like children, let us speak with simplicity, without understanding our Father's intentions. With complete faith in his goodness, let us say in our sorrow, but also in hope: "Our Father, who art in heaven, . . . your kingdom come, your will be done on earth as it is in heaven. Give us this day our daily bread and deliver us from all evil."

COMPARISON TABLE

Adult Funerals*

Readings from the Old Testament

	French Lectionary
English Lectionary	*(Fr. Roguet's Commentaries)*

Reading 1 = Reading 3
Reading 2 = Reading 5 (Wis 2:23, 3:1–6, 9)
Reading 3 = Reading 6 (Wis 4:7–14)
Reading 4 = Reading 7
Reading 5 = Reading 8
Reading 6 = Reading 9
Reading 7 = Reading 1

Readings from the New Testament

	French Lectionary
English Lectionary	*(Fr. Roguet's Commentaries)*

Reading 1 = Reading 10
Reading 2 = Reading 11 (Rom 5:6b–11)
Reading 3 = Reading 12
Reading 4 = Reading 13
Reading 5 = Reading 14 (Rom 8:14–23)
            also Reading 15 (Rom 8:18–23)
Reading 6 = Reading 16
Reading 7 = Reading 17
Reading 8 = Reading 20 (1 Cor 15:19–24a, 25–28)
Reading 9 = Reading 21
Reading 10 = Reading 23

Reading 11 = Reading 24 (Phil 3:20–4:1)
Reading 12 = Reading 25 (1 Thes 4:13–14, 17d–18)
Reading 13 = Reading 26
Reading 14 = Reading 28
Reading 15 = Reading 29 (1 Jn 3:14, 16–20)
Reading 16 = Reading 31
Reading 17 = Reading 32
Reading 18 = Reading 33

Gospels

	French Lectionary
English Lectionary	*(Fr. Roguet's Commentaries)*

Reading 1 = Reading 101
Reading 2 = Reading 102 (Mt 11:25–28)
Reading 3 = Reading 103
Reading 4 = Reading 104
Reading 5 = Reading 107 (Mk 15:33–34ac, 37–39, 16:1–6)
Reading 6 = Reading 109
Reading 7 = Reading 110 (Lk 12:35–38, 40)
Reading 8 = Reading 111 (Lk 23:33–34, 39–46, 50, 52–53)
Reading 9 = Reading 111 (same as above)
Reading 10 = Reading 112
Reading 11 = Reading 115
Reading 12 = Reading 116
Reading 13 = Reading 118
Reading 14 = Reading 119
Reading 15 = Reading 120 (Jn 12:24–28)
Reading 16 = Reading 121
Reading 17 = Reading 122 (Jn 17:1–3, 24–26)

Funerals of Baptized Children

Readings from the Old Testament

| | French Lectionary |
| English Lectionary | (Fr. Roguet's Commentaries) |

Reading 1 = Reading 59
Reading 2 = Reading 60

Readings from the New Testament

| | French Lectionary |
| English Lectionary | (Fr. Roguet's Commentaries) |

Reading 1 = Reading 61
Reading 2 = Reading 62
Reading 3 = Reading 63
Reading 4 = Reading 64
Reading 5 = Reading 65
Reading 6 = Reading 68
Reading 7 = Reading 69

Gospels

| | French Lectionary |
| English Lectionary | (Fr. Roguet's Commentaries) |

Reading 1 = Reading 123 (Mt 11:25–30)
Reading 2 = Reading 126
Reading 3 = Reading 116 (adult lectionary)
Reading 4 = Reading 128

Funerals of Unbaptized Children

First Readings

| | French Lectionary |
| English Lectionary | (Fr. Roguet's Commentaries) |

Reading 1 = Reading 71
Reading 2 = Reading 72

Gospel

The only gospel suggested in the English lectionary is Mark 15:33–46. Fr. Roguet gives a commentary on this gospel under reading 107 (Mk 15:33–34ac, 37–39, 16:1–6), p.

---

* Where there is any discrepancy in the selection of verses, the variation in the French lectionary is cited.

USEFUL NOTES

I. For Funerals of Adults (Anniversaries, Celebrations of the Word, etc.)

First Readings from the Old Testament

7. Isaiah 25:6a, 7–9. *God's victory over death*   34
The solid, simple text seems to fit any situation.

8. Lamentations 3:17–26. *From distress to hope*   35
This reading should be used at very emotional funerals: the death
of the family breadwinner, the death of a wife loved by everyone,
the death of an only son, etc.

9. Daniel 12:1b–3. *Belief in the resurrection*   37
The clarity of this brief reading and its Old Testament source allow
the proclamation of an important aspect of our faith, even when
there is a mixed congregation.

First Readings from the New Testament

10. Acts 10:34–43.* *Witness of the resurrection*   41
This text can easily be offered to any congregation. It contains the
essence of the Christian faith, especially by use of narrative, which
makes it more easily understood than some considerations that are
deeper and perhaps more abstract. This reading is kerygma, rather
than catechesis; it provides a remarkable summary of Jesus' life.
We see nothing to gain in adopting the Short Form, whose two
verses (!) omit a reminder of the entire gospel. Nevertheless, in
our commentary we have placed in parentheses whatever corresponds to the two verses.
For a congregation that will not follow very closely, we suggest two
minor modifications in the text. In the beginning, say "St. Peter,"
rather than "Peter." And in verse 39c, substitute "hanging him on
a cross" for "hanging him on a tree."

11. Romans 5:6b–11. *Christ has died for us*   42
Magnificent, moving text. Can it be grasped by an average congregation?

12. Romans 5:17–21. *Through Jesus, the New Adam, we have life*   44
The same remarks as for reading 11. For a better-informed congregation, it may be helpful to "demythologize" Adam's sin by showing that St. Paul regarded Christ's grace as primary and decisive.

13. Romans 6:3–9.* *Baptized in Christ's death and resurrection*   46
Despite its depth, this text is accessible to many. We can hear the
reading during the Easter Vigil and at a baptismal celebration.
Besides, the text is concretized by a well-known sacramental image

of baptism. Finally, the reading is related to several funeral liturgy prayers and to several funeral rituals (blessed water, Easter candle). Verses 5–7, omitted in the Short Form reading, offer little to the overall thought. Therefore our commentary fits both Long and Short forms.

14. Romans 8:14–17.   *We are God's children*   47
    The text seems to us to be very understandable, due to its references to the Lord's Prayer and to "God's children," a well-known idea.

15. Romans 8:18–23.   *There's a new world coming*   48
    This apparently difficult text is related to very modern preoccupations and seems to be understandable by a somewhat cultivated congregation.

16. Romans 8:31b–35, 37–39.   *Who will be able to separate us from Christ's love?*   50
    The vehemence and fervor of this beautiful reading seem to make it touching for everyone.

17. Romans 14:7–9, 10b–12.   *We belong to the Lord*   52
    In our opinion, this lovely text should be reserved for the funeral of a sincere Christian or for the celebration of the Word, with the Christian community present.

18. 1 Corinthians 15:1–5, 11.   *The good news*   54
    This reading contains the essential kerygma of apostolic teaching. We must not fear to proclaim it.

19. 1 Corinthians 15:12, 16–20.   *With Christ we will be raised up*   56
    This reading follows reading 18 and is its corollary. Our resurrection is an article of faith, which we must make known.

20. 1 Corinthians 15:19–24a, 25–28.   *The final victory over death*   58
    This text is so rich that we can surely understand the suggestion of a Short Form option. Nevertheless, we must regret that the Short Form lacks the verses that give a triumphal version of Christ's mission, which has reached its completion.

21. 1 *Corinthians* 15:51–54, 57.   *We will be raised in a transformed state*   60
    This text was frequently used in the pre-Vatican II liturgy, but, despite all that exposure, it is still a difficult text. We wonder whether using this text may raise more objections than we have time to answer. The reading depicts a worthwhile doctrine that cannot be called into question.

22. 2 Corinthians 4:14–5:1.   *Death and transfiguration*   62
    This splendid reading, which seems to be easily understood by the
    average Christian, is especially appropriate for the funeral of
    someone who has died after a long illness or painful injuries.

23. 2 Corinthians 5:1, 6–10.   *Toward the eternal dwelling place*   64
    A kind of parable filled with poetry. But can it touch those who are
    hardly believers?

24. Philippians 3:20–4:1.   *Our bodies are destined for glory*   65
    This brief and striking reading can interest many listeners and
    speak to prejudices which consider the Christian faith a disincar-
    nate spiritualism.

25. 1 Thessalonians 4:13–14, 17d–18.   *The heaven we believe in*   67
    A very salutary theme for those who are tempted by private
    "revelations," occultism, etc. On the other hand, the text challenges
    hopeless agnosticism.

26. 2 Timothy 2:8–13.   *The death of the apostle Paul*   69
    This text, which may appear excessive and unfit for the burial of
    an "average Christian," is very moving when used for a missionary
    or a militant whose death seems to be a setback for evangelization.

27. 1 Peter 1:3–8.   *Joy in time of trial*   71
    This thanksgiving hymn, which is bursting with optimism, may
    startle the congregation, unless it is a solid, believing congregation
    or unless the deceased, who may have been greatly tested during
    his or her life, died in great peace, nourished by hope.

28. 1 John 3:1–2.   *We are God's children*   73
    The remarks for reading 27 are also appropriate for this reading,
    although the aspect of "obscure faith" may have too much em-
    phasis.

29. 1 John 3:14, 16–20.   *Love enables us to pass from death to life*   75
    This reading is quite fitting for the funeral of a Christian who,
    though not exemplary in all respects, has shown much generosity
    and devotion.

30. 1 John 4:7–10.   *God is love*   77
    This statement is so often repeated, and seems so astonishing, that
    its application can be given even to what appears to be a poorly
    prepared congregation.

Gospels

172 HOMILIES FOR FUNERALS

105. Mark 10:28–30. *The reward for self-denial* 106
We should not consider reading such a gospel for the funeral of "just any" Christian. It must be reserved for a priest, brother, nun, or a militant who has truly spent himself or herself in evangelization.

106. Mark 14:32–34. *Jesus' prayer before his death* 109
It appears that this episode, which is profoundly human, can be appropriate for all funerals.

107. Mark 15:33–34ac, 37–39, 16:1–6. *Jesus died to live once again* 112
This simple, concrete gospel tells us about the central event of our faith. Thus it fits every occasion.

108. Luke 2:22b, 25–32. *"You can dismiss your servant in peace"* 115
This reading and its commentary are appropriate for an elder who has died with a peaceful faith.

109. Luke 7:11–17. *Jesus raises an only son from the dead* 118
It seems impossible to read the account of this miracle at a wake service in front of the casket; but the reading can be used for a funeral Mass and for an anniversary service.

110. Luke 12:35–38, 40. *"Keep yourselves ready"* 120
Like the parable of the ten young girls (reading 103), this reading is an exhortation to vigilance, which seems more appropriate for a celebration to *prepare* for death rather than for a funeral Mass. Nevertheless, it can be used in a funeral Mass because the tone is not severe.

111. Luke 23:33–34, 39–46, 50, 52–53. *We die with Jesus in order to be with him in paradise* 122
The remarks (offered above) for a section of St. Mark's Passion (reading 107) are equally valid here. But Mark's text gives a more global view of the Easter mystery. Luke's account has been selected to portray the mercy of the dying Jesus and the good thief's prayer, which Jesus answers.

112. Luke 24:13–35. *Stay with us. Evening is near* 123
The story is so beautiful that it can not only move a believing congregation but touch any listener in a deep way. Although the Lectionary suggests a Short Form reading, our commentary does not take that suggestion into account. The omitted verses are not indispensable. The parts of the commentary that concern the omitted verses can be understood despite the omission.

113. John 3:16–17. *God so loved the world* 127
With force and extreme brevity, this text is genuine kerygma. That's why it can be addressed to everyone with a brief commentary.

114. John 5:24–29. *Passing from death to life* 128
We can understand why this passage, which deals only with life and death, is in the Lectionary. But all exegetes recognize that "the dead" (in verse 25) should be taken in a metaphorical sense to designate sinners. The progression of thought disappears when we do violence to the text by allowing ourselves to believe that the entire text speaks of the physical dead. This is a text that should be studied within the whole context of the Gospel, but it is a very difficult text to preach on.

115. John 6:37–40. *"I will raise up everyone on the last day"* 130
The commentary develops and provides a special basis for the often misunderstood doctrine of bodily resurrection.

116. John 6:51–58. *"Whoever eats this bread will live forever"* 132
The text can be used only for a deceased person who went to Communion frequently, or at least regularly. The commentary explains the connection between eucharistic life and bodily resurrection. The explanation of the latter dogma, an abstraction from the Eucharist, is given in the commentary for reading 115.

117. John 10:14–16. *"There will be one flock, one shepherd"* 135
The commentary describes the shepherd's task of gathering sheep. Therefore we can use the text even for funerals of people who, in the course of their lives, hardly made a profession of belonging to the Church.

118. John 11:17–27. *"I am the resurrection"* 138
In a much shorter form (11:21–27), this gospel text was used for funerals in the old Missal. John 11:17–27 can be used often, because it describes a central datum of our faith. Nevertheless, it is more appropriate for a truly Christian family in which Jesus is considered a friend.

119. John 11:32b–45. *Jesus raises up his friend Lazarus* 139
As we said in our remarks for reading 109, this resurrection account does not appear to be appropriate for a funeral ceremony but, rather for a "Word celebration" or a service that is celebrated when "the body is absent"—for example, an anniversary Mass.
The omission of verses 37–40 (Short Form) does not affect our commentary.

120. John 12:24–28. *The grain that dies bears fruit*   141
   As indicated in the commentary, this is merely a parable. Death,
   of itself, is not the source of fruitfulness. Therefore the text can be
   used only for a deceased person who has led a genuine Christian
   life. The commentary, which clearly indicates the text proposed
   for the Short Form, corresponds to the division of Jesus' discourse,
   which is made up of two related but distinct themes.

121. John 14:1–6. *"I am the way, the truth, and the life"*   145
   The text is addressed to believers. But the salvation promise, contained in it, allows the text to be used extensively.

122. John 17:1–3, 24–26. *"I want them to be with me"*   147
   Despite the remarks in the first edition of the new Lectionary, the
   Short Form reading cannot begin with verse 24. We should retain
   the introduction, made up of the first three verses of the Long
   Form reading.
   Jesus' "priestly prayer" is composed of three parts: he prays for
   himself (verses 1–3 of the integral reading), for his disciples (vv.
   6–19), and finally "for those who will believe in me through their
   word" (v. 20). This last section constitutes the Short Form (vv.
   24–26). Despite its appearance, it seems best to reserve the reading
   for funerals of believers ("Those you have given me . . . these have
   known you have sent me").

123. John 19:17ab, 18, 25–30. *At the foot of Jesus' cross*   149
   In our commentary, we place more emphasis on the witnesses of
   Jesus' death than on the dying Jesus, and so it seems appropriate to
   use this reading for a deceased person who was not a perfect
   Christian by any means, but whose close survivors deeply believe
   (such as those especially attached to the Blessed Virgin, those who
   frequently pray the Rosary, pilgrims to Lourdes, etc.).

II. For Funerals of Baptized Children

First Readings from the Old Testament

64. Ephesians 1:3–5. *Blessed be God* 157
    A pericope proper to the lectionary for baptized children. The commentary (p. 157) has been redacted accordingly.

68. Revelation 7:9–10, 15–17. *God will dry every tear* 158
    A commentary proper to the lectionary for children, baptized or not. Commentary on p. 158

69. Revelation 21:1–3, 5a. *God himself will be with them* 82
    Compared with the reading for adults, the "infant version" omits verse 2, apparently for no good reason. "This is God's dwelling" (v. 3) points to the "new Jerusalem" (v. 2). The children's version stops before verses 6–7. Surely the reason for this is that a child cannot be someone "who thirsts." But "I will be his God and he shall be my son" might be very appropriate. The commentary, which insists on "being with," can still be applied to children.

124. Matthew 18:1–5, 10. *The greatest in the kingdom of heaven* 160
    A pericope proper to the lectionary for the burial of children. Commentary on p.

   The asterisk after a scriptural citation means the Lectionary suggests a Short Form reading for the text.

SUGGESTED READINGS FOR THE BURIAL OF UNBAPTIZED CHILDREN

For each reading, the first number refers to the adult lectionary, the second number to the lectionary for baptized children.

Earlier, we indicated the differences in the readings of similar pericopes in both the adult lectionary and the lectionary for baptized children. The readings that are common to the two lectionaries for children (baptized and unbaptized) have identical verses.

First Readings

70. Job 14. *A model of hope*, nos. 2 and 57
71. Isaiah 25. *God's victory over death*, nos. 7 and 59
7.2 Lamentations 3. *From distress to hope*, nos. 8 and 60
73. Romans 14. *We belong to the Lord*, nos. 17 and 62
74. 1 John 4. *"God is love,"* nos. 30 and 67
75. Revelation 7. *God will dry every tear*, no. 68
76. Revelation 21. *"God himself will be with them,"* nos. 33 and 69

Gospels

131. Matthew 11. *"Come to me all you who are weary,"* nos. 102 and 123
132. Matthew 18. *The greatest in the kingdom of heaven* (proper to the lectionary for children), no. 124
133. Mark 14. *Jesus' prayer before his death*, nos. 106 and 125
134. John 10. *"There will be one flock, one shepherd,"* nos. 117 and 127
135. John 11. *Jesus weeps for his friend, Lazarus*, sections taken from nos. 119 and 128
136. John 19. *At the foot of Jesus' cross*, nos. 122 and 130

APPENDIX

Readings at the Crematorium

For a long time, the Church has opposed cremation because in Nineteenth-century Europe certain associations advocated cremation as a profession of materialistic and antireligious belief. The Church retains its preference for the burial given to Jesus, a burial later practiced by early Christians so as to follow Jewish tradition and to distinguish Christians from pagans, who practiced incineration. But the Church accepts incineration, provided belief in the resurrection and belief in Jesus, the unique Mediator, are maintained. When these conditions are present, nothing prevents a funeral celebration in church and use of the funeral lectionary.

However, we can pre-read another ceremony "at the place of cremation," as indicated in the sections "In the Church" and "At the Grave" (nos. 37–57 of the funeral ritual).

You will also find in these ritual sections the indication of a "short reading." Thus the four following texts are proposed, which "will be read in such a manner that they can be meditated on at the same time."

Romans 8:18–21 (see first readings, no. 15, except for the last two verses. Commentary above, p. 48)
Creation, which suffers because of enslavement, will be liberated from that slavery in order to know the freedom and glory of God's children.

1 Corinthians 15:52b–54 (see first readings, no. 21, except the beginning and the last verse. Commentary above, p. 60)

John 6:39–40 (see gospel 115, except for the first two verses. Commentary above, p. 130)
Whoever believes in Jesus will be raised up by Jesus on the last day.

John 14:1–6 (gospel 121. Commentary above, p. 145)
"I am the way, the truth, and the life; no one comes to the Father but through me."

INDEX OF PRINCIPAL THEMES